STANLEY W. FISHER F.R.S.A.

British Pottery and Porcelain

D1475857

BELL PUBLISHING COMPANY · NEW YORK

TO MURIEL, MY WIFE

*The line illustrations which appear
throughout the text were drawn by
the author.*

This edition published by Bell Publishing Company, Inc,
a division of Crown Publishers, Inc.,
by arrangement with MacGibbon & Kee, Ltd.
A   B   C   D   E   F   G   H

Printed in the United States of America

Contents

Preface

IT is a long step from the days when a man's possessions were confined to the bare essentials of living to the present time when so many of the furnishings of a home are chosen not only for use but also because they are lovely to look at. At the same time, of course, not every home lover is a collector, and not every fortunate possessor of beautiful things has an expert knowledge of them, or even wishes to acquire such knowledge. Man's passion for collecting is indeed a strange phenomenon, and it is governed to a large extent by fashionable trends, even though it is initially motivated by an innate love of beauty, and by that desire to acquire which is probably an inheritance from those far-off days when hoarding in good times was essential to survival in the bad.

A very famous and wise connoisseur of fifty years ago, Sir James Yoxall, had something to say about people who 'would like to collect if they knew anything at all about it', and the purpose of this book is to meet that desire with practical suggestion and help. In the first place (and here perhaps I may be pardoned for expressing biased views), the collector of porcelain and pottery of any kind has an advantage over his fellow enthusiasts. Apart from its undeniable beauty, both of form and of applied decoration of so many fascinating kinds, it takes up comparatively little space even in modest homes, it enhances any piece of furniture upon which it is placed, and it has considerable human interest. It has been truly said that the study of ceramics is the study of mankind, because social history and customs through the years are so often mirrored in the styles and subjects of painted or printed decoration.

When once the possessor of a few pieces of family china feels the desire to know more about them, it is but a short step to supplement them with new acquisitions, and the question inevitably arises as to what sort of wares to collect. There are many possibilities, depending on personal taste and, of course, on the depth of the pocket. There are many who at first gather together a miscellany of specimens of every kind, British and foreign, decorated in any style, and though this sort of magpie collecting is usually but a prelude to something more selective, the experience gained, and even perhaps the mistakes made, are not entirely wasted. The process of 'weeding out' that which no longer appeals leaves behind the nucleus of something more worthwhile.

Lady Charlotte Schreiber, surely the most indefatigable and successful collector of all time, whose interest began late in life and who was able to pursue her quest throughout Europe at a time when porcelain and pottery were much less appreciated and understood than they are nowadays, had as her aim the bringing together of specimens representative of British ceramic art. She was not primarily interested in beauty and variety, but rather in full representation, and the modern collector, however wealthy, could not possibly hope to follow her example. Nevertheless, there are equally enjoyable and rewarding ways of collecting. A lover of fine painting might well concentrate upon specimens painted with landscapes, birds, flowers, heraldry or oriental designs, and quite unconsciously the development of style through the years, as fashions changed and as artists became more proficient, would add fresh and unforeseen interest. This very development is a fascinating thing in itself, and might well underlie the making of quite another kind of collection, whose specimens would illustrate the copying in turn, by artists feeling their way, of the decorative idiom of the Far East, Holland, Meissen and Sèvres, culminating in a nineteenth-century British style in which the decoration was all-important and the porcelain itself of secondary consideration.

Many collectors prefer to concentrate upon wares of one particular factory or group of factories, and they are sometimes influenced by prevailing market prices. Thus, when Worcester or Chelsea porcelain, or early Wedgwood jasper, for instance, are so fashionable that prices are high, it may well be that the wares of another factory are comparatively inexpensive. Every factory has had its vogue, and none remains out of fashion for very long. Then there is subdivision by period, which again introduces the question of cost, since by and large the early experimental wares are rare, while those of later origin are comparatively plentiful and still within the reach of the collector of modest means. Many of the shapes of pieces of domestic ware of the latter half of the eighteenth century, by far the most interesting period, are pleasing enough to demand specialization—the tea-poys, sucriers (or sugar basins), cream jugs, and tea-pots. In a collection of this kind variations in shape and decorative style suffice to prevent monotony, though it is clear that its specimens should be arranged in cabinets and not considered as incidental parts of a decorative scheme of furnishing. Specialization based upon decoration alone has many possibilities. Much of the earliest British porcelain was painted (and later printed) in cobalt blue applied under the protecting glaze, and 'blue and white', as it is commonly called, has a simple, unsophisticated appeal that has made many converts, apart from the fact that it blends admirably with oak furniture in particular. On a par with these wares, which were intended for everyday use and which were made in vast quantities, are those which were transfer-printed over the glaze in delicate red, puce, brown and black. They are delicate enough, and their patterns sufficiently varied, to have attracted the attention of collectors and students. On the other hand, if the attraction of colour is paramount, there is a wide choice indeed, and wares decorated in the distinctive styles of China, Japan and the Continent all have their devotees.

The earthenware collector, perhaps, is more likely to specialize, if only because there is such wide difference between the various bodies, glazes and styles of decoration used by the earthenware makers. The early wares of Whieldon, for example, covered with translucent coloured glazes, have an entirely different appeal from that of the clear-cut austerity of Wedgwood's jaspers and cream-wares. A lover of Pratt's well-nigh miraculous coloured prints on pot-lids or mugs might despise the same potter's moulded jugs, crudely painted in somewhat muddy enamels. Each collector must find his own preference, and set his own personal standard of beauty, and no printed word can do other than indicate the possibilities, and suggest the virtues of each particular kind of ware.

It is rare to find the average collector including figures among his specimens. They are somewhat apart, belonging as they do to a separate branch of ceramic art which is often more closely related to sculpture than to potting. Indeed, in Europe the first Meissen figures, made about 1731, were modelled upon the works of a sculptor, Johann Joachim Kaendler, and were looked upon as an important branch of his work and of that of his fellows. These, of course, were made of porcelain, and were imitated in this country, whereas figures of earthenware, made by such potters as Astbury and Whieldon, were much less sophisticated, crudely modelled, and traditionally English in style. Apart from the dictates of personal preference, the decision to collect early figures, of whatever kind, must inevitably be influenced by the fact that they are rare and expensive. What is more, they have always been reproduced to such an extent that a beginner is all too easily liable to be deceived.

It will be clear from the foregoing remarks that china collecting can take many forms, but naturally enough there can be keen interest without serious collecting. As has already been said, one may already possess a few family pieces, and desire perhaps to supplement them with others which may help to furnish the home, a vase here and there, a few plates upon a dresser, and perhaps a small cabinet of interesting pieces. As distinct from this, collecting implies study. But, however it may be, pride of possession is undoubtedly enhanced by knowledge, which can be acquired in several ways. Museums, of course. Not only in the British and South Kensington Museums, but also in the provincial ones the finest examples of every kind of ware are to be seen, the only disadvantage being that it is necessary to handle in order fully to learn. Mere admiration is not enough, although it can teach shapes and patterns. On the other hand, every collector loves nothing better than to show his treasures to a fellow enthusiast, whether he be a beginner or not, when they may be examined at leisure. Similarly, those who are able to join a Ceramic Circle not only learn much from discussion and from lectures by experts, but also savour what is surely the fullest enjoyment and benefit of any hobby, talking about it with those who understand.

Lastly, there is the printed word, in the form of magazines and books. Every journal devoted to antiques has regular articles on ceramics, and the first books dealing with the subject were published in this country about eighty years ago. It is natural, therefore, that the collector has hundreds of books at his disposal, which may be borrowed from a library or purchased new or second-hand. Some are out of print, and may be out of date, although such books as Jewitt's *Ceramic Art of Great Britain*, published as long ago as 1877, are still valuable because so many of the wares described were actually being made at that time, or had been made at factories then only recently closed down. That kind of book is therefore authoritative. There are more recent books, some for the general collector, some for popular reading, some elementary, and some advanced. Some deal with the entire range of British pottery or porcelain, while others describe in greater detail the wares of one particular factory or style. And we must not forget that the British V. & A. Museums have always issued inexpensive but excellent handbooks describing their own great collections.

Every collector wonders, at the beginning, how best to acquire fine pieces, and it may be well to suggest, at this point, that the days of bargains are well-nigh at an end. Indeed, fine-quality porcelain and pottery have almost as fixed a price as any other popular commodity, and that is why buying from a reputable dealer has much to recommend it. He is prepared to guarantee what he sells, and his price (which includes the price of his experience and of his effort in finding his goods) is a recognized one. Nevertheless, half the pleasure in collecting must be in 'hunting', and prizes may still be found in unlikely places. What of auction sales? Sothebys and Christie's, and the other famous London rooms naturally offer the widest choice, and one can buy in a comparatively comfortable and quiet atmosphere, apart from the fact that no one knows how an auction sale should be conducted who has not visited them. And there is another point which is not generally appreciated. Whereas at a country sale a single good piece may arouse great interest, and so stimulate fierce competition, in a London sale room half the lots, perhaps, are of very high quality and so fetch high prices, whereas the rest may be average in comparison and so may be bought most reasonably. It is not every collector who can afford to buy the exceptional, though at the same time it is better, from the outset, to purchase a single piece of good quality rather than several inferior ones. It is a mistake for the general public to imagine that goods cannot be bought if dealers are present at a sale. Unless he has a commission a dealer will not pay a silly price. At the same time, if he is pushed he may well make prices so high, in his endeavour to buy stock, that the private buyer would have done better to allow him to buy the lots, and to purchase them from him afterwards. The psychology of buying at auction is a strange phenomenon. No one has ever been able to understand why some collectors are willing to buy at auction at prices they would not think of paying to a reputable dealer who is prepared to guarantee his goods, and who sells with them the benefit of his knowledge and experience.

Proper viewing of the goods offered at an auction sale is essential. It is surprising how easy it can be to overlook cracks or other defects, and modern restorers are remarkably clever. There is no redress if faults are discovered after a lot has been knocked down. There are mixed opinions as to whether damaged pieces are ever worth buying. A true rarity, whether unashamedly cracked or skilfully repaired, may be a sensible 'buy' if cost has to be considered, but anything else will never fully satisfy. Moreover, when a similar but perfect specimen comes along, as one day it will, the damaged one will probably prove to be worth practically nothing. A true collector buys his treasures because he cannot resist them, but at the same time there is always the knowledge that wise buying is an investment. The purpose of this book is to attempt to meet the early needs of the average collector, in both regards.

Bewdley, Worcestershire   STANLEY W. FISHER

CHAPTER ONE

Introduction

THERE is no record of the beginnings of what must be among the earliest of all man's handicrafts, the making of vessels of clay. We do not know when baking in the sun gave place to firing in ovens or kilns, or when and where the potter's wheel was invented. Through the centuries the potter's craft was developed, until three main classes of ware emerged which we call earthenware, stoneware and porcelain, and which may very often share each other's characteristics to a greater or lesser degree, depending upon such factors as content of ingredients and firing temperatures. For instance, though both earthenware and stoneware are made of clay alone, the higher firing necessary to make the latter gives it a much greater vitrification and hardness, and occasionally a degree of that translucency which is more usually a characteristic of porcelain. Porcelain, of whatever variety, is made of some kind of clay with the addition of other ingredients. Since a vessel of fired clay may be as porous as an ordinary flower-pot, it is usually given a protective skin of glaze, which is really a kind of glass.

The study of the very early pottery made in Neolithic days, or even of the fine wares made by the Romans in this country, is more the concern of the archaeologist than of the collector. With the coming of the Normans nomadic potters began to make wares of yellow, green and brown crudely decorated with whatever kind of tool that came to hand; they 'impressed' designs in the soft clay with sea-shells, 'incised' them with sharp flints or bits of stick, or added 'applied' ornament in the form of small pads of clay in a wide variety of shapes. But these medieval wares, too, are more becomingly housed in a museum, and our interest properly begins when we meet what are known as the 'slip-wares' of the seventeenth century.

This kind of ware was made at many centres, notably in

London, Cheshire, Derbyshire, Kent (at Wrotham) and Stafford-shire. The most representative and certainly the best known of the slip-wares are associated with the Toft family of Staffordshire, whose name appears in the border design of many valuable dishes or platters of large size. Pieces are known bearing the names of both Thomas and Ralph, though neither is recorded as a potter, so that it has often been suggested that they were the recipients and not the makers. If that were so, one can only marvel that they received so many fine presents. Whoever was responsible for the making, slip-ware is characteristically English, vigorous rather than beautiful, unsophisticated, and setting a standard in the restrained use of plastic clay. The body of the ware was coarse red clay, upon which the 'slip', a creamy, white mixture of clay and water, was applied in lines and dots, just as a confectioner ices a cake. The designs featured heraldry, portraits, figures and busts, animals and birds, flowers, and trellis-work, and the whole was protected by thick lead glaze, which had the effect of mellowing the colours.

Although slip-ware was made well into the nineteenth century (so that pieces of it are often dug out from our gardens from just below the surface), its weight and clumsiness made it unsuited to everyday domestic use, and it was gradually ousted by stone-wares which were introduced towards the end of the seventeenth century. Stonewares were alien to this country in that they were made to copy Böttger's Meissen imitations of Chinese stoneware by John and David Elers, and by John Dwight of Fulham. Elers ware may be black or red, sometimes turned in the lathe, or sometimes bearing applied ornament which was stamped out in metal dies. Since the Elers body was highly vitrified it was not necessary to glaze it, so that the detail of the applied decoration is always clear and sharp. In contrast, when another famous potter, John Astbury, made similarly designed wares of ordinary earthenware, around the middle of the eighteenth century, his applied reliefs of vine pattern and other small ornaments were stamped out from contrasting white clay, and he glazed his ware.

During the first half of the seventeenth century stoneware was further developed by covering it with 'salt glaze', the salt being thrown into the kiln at a temperature of over 2,000° Fahrenheit. The first wares so treated were white, in the Elers style, but later on they were moulded in various styles, incised with blue-filled designs or, most beautifully, enamelled in jewel-like colours. Salt-glazed stoneware has never gone out of production, though it is now used almost entirely for industrial purposes and does not clearly show the slightly pitted, orange-skin surface that is so admired by collectors.

Astbury's continuance of the old tradition of lead-glazed earthenware was copied by others, including Whieldon, Wedgwood, and the Woods. Whieldon, and Astbury too, made figures more notable for 'quaintness' than beauty, Whieldon made his famous 'tortoiseshell' wares, with Wedgwood he made beautifully moulded 'cauliflower' domestic ware, and the Woods made Toby Jugs and figures the modelling of which often nearly approached the spirit and finish of the porcelain models they sometimes tried to rival. But despite the clean nature of stoneware and the sturdy homeliness of the lead-glazed earthenwares, the ever more plentiful Chinese porcelain that had been appearing in Europe for many years inspired our potters to make something like it, and their answer took the form of delft. This was a tin-glazed, white surfaced earthenware, and it was not, of course, translucent. Nevertheless, it had the superficial appearance of porcelain, even though its powdery surface before firing necessitated the use of very bold, unhesitant brushwork. So, in London, Bristol and Liverpool, potters made delft, while their fellows in Italy made majolica, and in Germany and Spain made faience, all of it colourful, and much of it decorated in porcelain styles.

Broadly speaking, the collector may devote his attention to any of these succeeding classes of pottery—lead-glazed wares, stoneware, and delft—and to any one or more of the innumerable kinds of eighteenth- and nineteenth-century earthenwares which will be described later in greater detail, the lustred wares, the ironstones, and the ordinary ware which is interesting only by virtue of the kinds of decoration applied to it. There is endless scope, and there is something to suit every taste and every purse.

The earliest porcelain was made by the Chinese, probably during the T'ang dynasty, between A.D. 618 and 906, and it was thereafter steadily developed under State management until it reached the peak of technical and decorative excellence during the K'ang Hsi period (1662–1722). It was the fine ware made then that found its way to England, and it was natural that Western potters tried to rival it, by making delft and by striving to discover the carefully preserved secret of its whiteness and translucency. The first attempts, wherever made, were almost certainly based upon the transparency of glass, and the first continental porcelain, made in Florence about 1580, was made of clay mixed with a sort of powdered glass which we call 'fritt'. Similar porcelains, now given the obvious name of 'artificial' because they were not made according to the Chinese formula, which used only china-stone (petuntse) and china-clay (kaolin), were made later at Rouen (1673), St Cloud, Chantilly and Mennecy.

All these early 'soft-pastes', as they are alternatively called, have an entirely different, more mellow appearance from the Chinese ware, and they are so lovely that it is perhaps difficult to understand just why the continental (and, later, our own) chemists persevered in their endeavours to make 'hard-paste' or true porcelain. At any rate, the world-famous pottery at Meissen, near Dresden, was founded in 1710, after the secret had at long last been discovered by a German nobleman named Schirnhausen and his assistant Böttger, and the porcelain made there was supreme throughout Europe until during the latter half of the eighteenth century, when the fritt-paste wares of Sèvres, always a dangerous rival, ousted it from favour.

In our own country the early attempts, unlike those which were made on the Continent, were left to private enterprise. The most unlikely and, one would think, unpractical people, even Samuel Johnson, made their experiments, often using such unpromising ingredients as powdered egg-shells and glue. At length, in 1744, Thomas Frye and Edward Heylyn of Bow took out a patent, porcelain was made at Chelsea even perhaps a little earlier, and between then and about 1770 factories were established at Bristol, Worcester, Plymouth, Derby, Longton Hall, Caughley (pronounced Calfley), Lowestoft and Liverpool. At all except Plymouth the first wares were of the artificial or 'soft-paste' variety, and made according to quite different formulae, which resulted in their having different appearances and translucencies. It was William Cookworthy whose discovery of china-clay in Cornwall led to the first English making of true porcelain, at Plymouth. That was in 1768, and in 1770 the business moved to Bristol (a centre twenty years earlier of 'soft-paste' making) and thence, about eleven years later, to New Hall in Staffordshire.

The collector's interest in these early wares is mainly due, one might say, to their imperfections, for their makers relied on their own endeavours and were always experimenting. Each early fritt-paste, and each glaze has its own characteristics which reveal themselves to the practised eye in the forms of translucencies of different colour, varying opacity, firing cracks, traces of imperfectly mixed or fritted ingredients, warping, discoloration and so on. One can trace the slow improvement in the quality and variety of enamels, and the gradual development of decorative style as the artists copied in turn from the Chinese, from delft and from Meissen and Sèvres wares. Such factors as these arouse the interest, and when in the early nineteenth century a Spode paste containing a large proportion of bone-ash was generally adopted throughout the industry, porcelains were made which were technically perfect, but which at the same time are of less interest to the connoisseur.

There have always been potters who were not content to follow the herd, and we find that in the 1820s porcelains intended to rival the finest soft-paste Sèvres were made at Nantgarw and Swansea, at Madeley in Shropshire, and elsewhere. Many of them, as we shall see, were invented by a master chemist, potter and decorator named William Billingsley. And, of course, there were the many experimental pastes of the great Worcester factories of Flights and Chamberlains, the wares made at Coal-port which for some time followed the Welsh tradition because Billingsley went from Wales to Shropshire, taking his recipes with him, and the contemporary Rockingham porcelain which was technically excellent, but which was so expensively decorated that it cost too much to produce.

So much for the story of the development of china making in Britain, albeit treated perforce in a somewhat inadequate way. There are many by-paths and diversions which the collector will find for himself, if he reads enough, and if he examines enough specimens. What has been said is purely introductory.

CHAPTER TWO

Chelsea porcelain

CHELSEA porcelain was made for the fashionable world of London Society, and even today the name somehow recalls the graciousness of a Georgian village which was once famous as the haunt of many famous men (and infamous for its footpads), and which even now is popularly associated with half-forgotten by-ways and courts, quiet and secluded, which retain something of their former exclusiveness. There is still magic in the name of Chelsea.

The porcelain itself may be conveniently divided into four main classes, as follows:

1. The first period of the incised triangle and the raised anchor marks, the 1740s.
2. The period of (at first) the raised anchor and the red anchor marks, the 1750s.
3. The period of the gold anchor mark, the 1760s.
4. The Chelsea-Derby period, the 1770s.

These divisions are arbitrary, for the characteristics of the paste, glaze and decoration, and the use of the several marks, have no clear-cut boundaries, chronological or otherwise.

The early history of the factory shares with those of others an uncertainty which need not worry us unduly. The wares are more important than the men who made them, but of these a silversmith from Liège, named Nicholas Sprimont, was the man who as manager put the factory on a firm footing soon after 1742. As he was a silversmith it follows that many early jugs, salt-cellars and small vases were modelled from silver originals— the famous 'goat and bee' jug is a case in point, in both white and enamelled forms—while at the same time he naturally had a bias towards continental styles which, fortunately for the factory's success, were in great favour in this country. Their graciousness and frippery charmed the wealthy dilettanti and the solid London tradesman alike. Indeed, considerable effort was made to obtain foreign porcelain to serve as models, mostly from Meissen and Sèvres. Lord Chesterfield sent a little snuff-box to Paris, and in his covering letter, dated 9th August 1750 he

Figure 1. Chelsea 'goat and bee' jug.

remarked, 'I send it to you merely to let you see how well we imitate the Dresden china, and for less than a quarter of the price.' On the other hand, when two years later he received a gift of French porcelain, he had to change his tune, and wrote, 'It is charming, beautiful, and beats our manufacture all to nothing. I have shown it to the manager, who was quite provoked and begged hard that I would lend it him for a few days for a pattern. I could not refuse him.' Such documentary evidence as this indicates very clearly that the patronage of Society was most necessary to the Chelsea management, and indeed to the managements of all our early factories, even though it meant that they were under an obligation to produce a great deal of quite unpractical ware.

Sprimont probably made use of a reliable recipe for making porcelain, a recipe which belonged to his partner, Charles Gouyn, and which it is supposed made better ware than that which was made at the very beginning by a workman from Derby named Thomas Briand. The improved porcelain much resembles milky-white glass which by transmitted light (that is, when held against a very strong electric light) shows tiny pinpricks of greater translucency. The glaze is very thick, glassy, sometimes like ivory in tone, but sometimes pure white due to the presence of tin oxide, and sometimes full of bubbles and tiny cracks. The factory mark was an incised triangle, rarely with a date, and it is important to remember that it is sometimes found on reproductions of the 'goat and bee' jug made at Coalport. Fortunately, however, it was added later, scratched through the glaze and not, of course, incised into the unbaked body beneath, as it ought to be. Examination under a magnifying-glass will reveal the difference. A great deal of the early ware was left 'in the white', notably pieces bearing moulded relief designs of prunus, tea-plant, vine and rose, for the elegant silver shapes and careful modelling needed no added embellishment. Enamelling, when found, is usually very simple. The Chelsea custom of covering defects such as bubbles in the glaze or firing-cracks with little painted leaves or insects is revealed on these, as well as on later pieces. The collector can learn much from a study of contemporary catalogues of the sales which were periodically held by the factory proprietors, and from press advertisements which were published after 1749.

Though most Chelsea porcelain of this period was influenced by German and French fashions, a notable exception may be seen in the figures of birds which bear the mark of an anchor cushioned upon a tiny, raised oval pad of clay. Whereas the famous Meissen birds were modelled by Kaendler from nature, the Chelsea modellers were inspired by the engravings in George

Edwards's *History of Uncommon Birds*, with the result that they
are apt to be rather stiff and formal in appearance.

Probably the best-known wares of the red anchor period are
also the rarest and the most valuable, the so-called 'Chelsea
Toys' of which George II, a patron of the factory, was an ardent
admirer and collector. These little gems of modelling, in the
forms of boxes, scent-flasks, *étuis* and trinkets of all kinds,
originated at Meissen, and a feature of them all is the exquisite

Figure 2. Chelsea scent-bottle and patchbox 'harlequin'.

miniature-like painting and inscribed mottoes and messages in
most curious French. The smallest are less than an inch in
height. The red anchor period was undoubtedly the best in the
history of the factory, and the colours used in every kind of
decoration, but in particular the bouquets and little sprays of
flowers, and insects, were smooth and pastel-like, with a very
sparing use of gilding. These flowers were also inspired by
Meissen, as indeed were most of the decorative styles, the
German modified Japanese 'Imari' and Chinese 'Japan' patterns,
and the landscapes. Jefferyes Hamett O'Neale (1734–1801),

usually called the 'Fable Painter', was an artist who painted fable subjects as depicted in Francis Barlow's *Aesop's Fables* and John Ogilby's *Fables of Aesop paraphrased in Verse*, modified to fit cups, saucers, dishes and plates. Equally desirable, and of course equally rare, are the wonderful plates painted with 'botanical flowers' or 'Hans Sloane' flowers, Sloane being the distinguished botanist of that time.

The paste of which such fine wares were made is 'harder' (and was probably more easily managed) than that of the first period. Instead of pin-pricks we find larger extra-translucent patches called 'moons', and three or four 'spur marks' beneath the bases of plates and dishes, small projecting knobs which show where the ware rested on little stands in the kiln. The glaze still seems to be very thick and glassy, sometimes crackled, often black-spotted, but soft-looking.

The red-anchor figures were again mostly copied from Meissen models, either exactly or modified, though the general sharp effect of the rococo modelling of the originals is much softened and mellowed by the use of the creamy Chelsea paste. Colours are restrained, and gold used sparingly, but about 1758 the Chelsea chemists began to mix bone-ash in the paste, with a view to strengthening it. So it undoubtedly did, with the result that much more ambitious figures and groups could be made. We find such large groups as the 'Music Lesson' and the 'Roman Charity', with a riot of bright colour, a profusion of gold, and the extravagant use of rococo scrolling. The new gold-anchor paste has fewer defects, the glaze is clear and glassy, but we often find that it has collected into thick, greenish, crazed pools in the hollows, say, between the rims and bottoms of plates and dishes, and in the crevices of figures. For domestic wares the artists turned to Sèvres for inspiration, imitating particularly the splendid ground colours which included a strong claret known as 'Rose Pompadour' and the Bleu-de-Roi which was re-named 'Mazarin Blue'. These colours are seen to best advantage when exotic and naturalistic birds, fruit, flowers, 'Chinese' figures, and figure subjects after Watteau and Boucher are reserved upon them. Another characteristic and most magnificent style of the period features fine polychrome flower painting in conjunction with brilliant tooled gilding, usually in the form of idealized golden pheasants, upon wide borders of the mazarine blue. There was every excuse for the old theory that the gold anchor denoted not so much a period, as the decorative quality of the ware.

In 1770 the Chelsea factory was taken over by Derby, and the period lasted until 1783. Under the hard-headed, businesslike Duesbury the old days of flippancy came to an end, for his aim was to produce more restrained wares for a wider, less cultured market. In this, of course, he much resembled Wedgwood, for his rather severe, classical style reflected the change in social life and outlook that foreshadowed the Industrial Revolution. So, although many of the old Chelsea figure moulds were retained, most of the domestic ware more closely resembled Derby, with a similar pale yellow translucency, though still retaining a soft, thick glaze. The Sèvres influence continued, with its characteristic festoons and flower-sprays, and some fine blue and white was made. This latter style of decoration was seldom attempted during the earlier Chelsea periods, possibly because it was considered to be too utilitarian, but the Chelsea-Derby painting was quite as good as that done at Worcester. On the whole the enamels are inferior to those used during the preceding gold-anchor period. The collector will have little difficulty in finding representative pieces, which include barrel-shaped mugs, ribbed, with loop handles, and nautilus shell-shaped sauce-boats or cream jugs, sparingly decorated with naturalistic flowers in pale colours.

CHAPTER THREE

Bow porcelain

IF the Chelsea workmen and artists were fanciful, it is equally true to say that those who worked at Bow held their own against their neighbouring rivals by producing wares that were practical and acceptable to the man-in-the-street. They were not, apparently, concerned so much with the whims of polite society; they concentrated on 'blue and white', they made large services of a sturdy paste, stoutly potted, that was astonishingly difficult to crack, and with few exceptions their styles of decoration were restrained.

As in the case of Chelsea, the events of the early years of the Bow factory are unrecorded. It has been surmised that work was begun as early as 1730, but in fact it was not until 1744 that Thomas Frye, an engraver and artist, and Edward Heylyn, a glass-maker, applied for a patent for the making of porcelain at Stratford-by-Bow. In 1748 there was a second patent, when two merchants named Weatherby and Crowther joined the concern, and two years later a new factory, called 'New Canton' was opened, which continued to operate until Duesbury bought everything up in 1776.

The unusual strength and weight of the porcelain was due in part to the use of bone-ash in the paste, in the form of calcined bones. This ingredient was responsible also for the marked opacity of much Bow porcelain, which is quite often completely resistant to the strongest transmitted light, and so can easily be mistaken for earthenware. There were several changes in the formula over the years, for whereas the first glossy porcelain included a proportion of pipe-clay, this appears to have been replaced, about 1755, by ground-up Chinese porcelain, while from about 1760 onwards the body was very similar to that used at Chelsea. The Bow glaze of the early years is opaque and milky because it had a high china-clay content. It was, in fact, a modification of the paste itself, but after 1749 a lead glaze was substituted which is much more transparent and has a greenish tinge in hollows and crevices, which is a most valuable aid to identification. It is this lead content which is the cause of a marked iridescence and of the patchy brown discoloration which is characteristic of much Bow ware. In passing, however, it should be mentioned that an all-over brown discoloration on either earthenware or porcelain is due to quite a different cause—the damage caused by leaving it in an oven.

Figure 3. Bow white mug with applied sprigged ornament.

One of the most interesting kinds of early Bow was made in imitation of the white Chinese blanc-de-chine or Fukien porcelain. The same kind of ware, decorated with applied sprigs of prunus or hawthorn, had already been copied on the Continent at St Cloud, Chantilly and Meissen, but the Bow variety gains in appearance by the mellow, almost oily nature of its glaze. It is in fact often quite yellow in contrast with the snowy whiteness of the foreign ware.

A considerable amount of Bow was painted in underglaze cobalt-blue, in imitation of the popular Chinese 'Blue Nankin' that had been imported into this country throughout the century.

The collector may with fair certainty ascribe it to the period before about 1755. The reason for this, as we shall understand in a later chapter, was because the Worcester factory, helped when necessary by the neighbouring works at Caughley, were able to establish a virtual monopoly of this cheaply produced class of porcelain. Strangely enough, underglaze blue-printed wares were hardly attempted at all, though the related process of printing in overglaze black or brick red was understood and practised. So far as blue and white is concerned, a favourite and

Figure 4. Bow bowl painted in underglaze blue with 'jumping boy' pattern.

fairly common design, used particularly for dishes and plates, features moulded vine-leaves and fruit, painted in powder-blue on a white ground. We often find octagonal, plain round, or wavy-edged plates decorated with Chinese landscapes in fan-shaped and round reserves on a powder-blue ground, and the peony was a much-favoured motif, both in underglaze blue and in enamels. The Bow bell-shaped mugs are quite different from those made at Worcester. They are heavily potted, often with a substantial ring at the base, they usually have heart-shaped lower handle terminals, and elaborate borders in the Chinese style were painted outside their rims. Among the most common blue-painted patterns are the 'Jumping Boy' (also found on Liverpool wares, and featuring a boy seated on a bank), the 'Image' (a warrior carrying a weapon over his shoulder), and the 'Lady playing on a Koto'. It is important to note that blue-painted Bow porcelain often has a marked greenish translucency owing to the admixture of cobalt in the paste itself. The reason for this was that the normal creamy tone was unacceptable to customers who had become accustomed to the characteristic grey-blue colour of the Oriental 'Blue Nankin' wares.

Apart from a few rare exceptions, such as a lovely design featuring Watteau figures in landscapes within a mazarine border scrolled with heavy gold, Bow polychrome decoration never made any attempt to rival the Chelsea splendour. Indeed, although some of the Chelsea painters moved to Bow in 1756, it is probable that prior to that date the more ambitious painting was done by outside decorators to whom the ware was sent 'in the white'. Nevertheless, there is much to admire in the simpler Bow styles, most of them inspired by the Japanese 'Kakiemon' patterns. Among them we find the 'Wheatsheaf' and the 'Quail' (or 'Partridge'), painted in clear, thick, raised enamels in a manner which imitates very closely the graceful drawing of the oriental originals. When Chinese decoration was copied it was usually either of the 'famille verte' or 'famille rose' class. While designs belonging to the former are invariably finely pencilled, almost delicate, those of the latter are somewhat more coarsely rendered in a distinctive palette of good rose-pink, pale green, pale opaque blue and aubergine. These are perhaps seen at their best in conjunction with the sprigged prunus blossoms already mentioned, and they are indeed almost peculiar to the factory, as was a strong 'sealing-wax red', dry and muddy, which was derived from iron oxide.

If we except the very early Bow figures, which were often very imperfect, clumsily modelled, crudely coloured, and yet full of strong, vigorous line, the Bow productions compare very favourably with those made at Chelsea. In fact, it is highly probable that workmen from the latter factory were responsible for them. At the same time the early specimens often have a clearness of outline that was the result of the use by the repairer (figure maker) of a sharp knife upon the folds of drapery or the outline of limbs. This process was evidently not applied to the smoother, more rounded Chelsea figures. Both factories made use of the same foreign models from time to time, but in order to distinguish the Bow versions we look for the typical pedestal base raised on four scrolled feet picked out in colour, a square or triangular hole low down at the back of large figures, a small round hole in the round bases of smaller ones, and the tell-tale greenish accumulations of glaze in the crevices. Tearings in the base are fairly common, but are not of course confined to Bow pieces.

Among the most attractive early figures are the white ones featuring stage personalities, among them the 'Fine Lady' and 'Fine Gentleman' (Kitty Clive and Woodward), taken from painted portraits, and the curious 'Sphinx' modelled after Pegg Woffington. It is possible that these were modelled by Roubiliac, though of this there is no real proof.

When figures are marked we find the anchor and dagger in red, or in red and blue, and the same mark was sometimes used on later domestic wares. It is on the blue-painted ware, however, that marks were more commonly used. Rarest of all is a script capital G, in overglaze blue. On powder-blue pieces we expect to find five or six simulated Chinese characters which are quite unlike those used on similar wares made at Worcester and Caughley, and workmen's numerals are commonplace. One underglaze blue-painted mark calls for special mention, the TF monogram which was once considered to be the initials of Thomas Frye, but which was actually a corrupted version of the Chinese character signifying jade. Accordingly, when the truth of the matter was understood and accepted, pieces so marked were ascribed to Worcester, in keeping with every other characteristic of paste, glaze and decoration.

CHAPTER FOUR

Worcester porcelain

THE original Worcester company was formed in 1751 to take over from an existing concern in Redcliffe Backs, Bristol, and it is the only one among all our pioneer manufactories which has enjoyed an unbroken history up to the present day. Moreover, although other English porcelains may by some collectors be rated higher for certain kinds of decoration or for their pastes or glazes, it is always Worcester that in the end is accepted as the yardstick of excellence by which others are judged.

There is no doubt that the factory started with advantages enjoyed by no other early concern. The fourteen signatories to the original deed of partnership, dated 4th June 1751, included Dr John Wall, the enthusiastic amateur with valuable connexions in the neighbourhood, William Davis, who one suspects was always the driving force, and who was a chemist by profession, Samuel Bradley, a goldsmith and silversmith, and other directors who were quite content to contribute their shares of the subscribed capital of £4,500. But above all, the partners were able to purchase, not only an already existing company (several of whose expert workmen were quite willing to go to Worcester), but also a workable formula which had already produced a beautiful, durable ware which was resistant to hot water—a most valuable selling-point among the tea-drinking gentry.

The new factory was established in Warmstry House (near to the River Severn and but recently demolished) and it was given the name of the 'Worcester Tonquin Manufacture'. It was publicly announced on 24th July 1752 that the whole 'Business' of the Bristol factory was to be carried on at the new premises. What do we know, to begin with, about the earlier concern? Unfortunately, not very much, for a great deal of research still has to be done. The site at Redcliffe Backs was somewhere in the dock area, and because the actual building was formerly a glass-house known as 'Lowdin's', the porcelain itself was once called 'Lowdin's Bristol', although it is now known that its proprietor, William Lowdin, had nothing to do with porcelain making. On the other hand, a brass-founder named Benjamin Lund was granted a licence to quarry soapstone at Gew Graze, near Mullion, in 1748. Now, soapstone, as we shall see, was an important ingredient of the Bristol (and Worcester) paste, and on the strength of this and other documentary evidence, it is reasonable to call the Bristol ware 'Lund's Bristol'.

It must be obvious that the work of porcelain making was interrupted as little as possible by the removal to Worcester, and it follows that there can be no way of distinguishing between the wares made round about that time, in either city. The paste was of course, of the 'fritt' variety and it contained a large proportion of soapstone, steatite, or 'soapy rock', as it was then called. The body it afforded was 'harder' than any other contemporary one, the glaze is usually very glossy but occasionally quite matt, and it is often filled with tiny bubbles which are visible where it has collected in pools, usually beneath the foot-rim. The glaze used on the blue and white ware was blued, and no Worcester glaze, of whatever period or kind, ever shows any sign of crazing, so well suited was it to the body beneath. By transmitted light the ware made during the first twenty years or so shows green, a very pure, bright green, though a yellowish tinge, particularly on later wares, may quite commonly be seen. After all, experiment never ceased, and in the study of porcelain the colour translucency test is never infallible.

Certain Bristol productions, a mere handful of sauce-boats, bear the embossed marks of 'Bristoll', 'Bristol' or 'Wigorn', and many others resemble them closely enough to be classed with them. Some have elevated rococo scrolled handles and festoons of flowers in relief, and are either white or else are painted in underglaze cobalt blue or coloured enamels. Others, of silver shape, white or coloured, have moulded panels and relief scroll-work. The painted designs are always in the Chinese style.

Apart from these classes of ware, which are certainly identifiable, we ascribe to Bristol and very early Worcester certain small hexagonal bottles, delicately painted with birds, flowers, or 'wheatsheaf' patterns, some large vases and covers, and a few tea-pots, octagonal or round. The decoration upon them all is again Chinese in style, because the first china painters had no tradition of their own, and so were obliged to copy from Chinese wares or, of course, from any other ware, including delft, which had imitated them. Furthermore, their customers expected that kind of decoration, knowing no other, and as far as the actual enamelling was concerned there was no great difficulty. The

Figure 5. 'Fritt-paste' Bristol.

technique differed little from that of enamelling on metal. The difficulty was to make an acceptable porcelain, not to decorate it.

Worcester enamels were good from the beginning, brilliant, seldom muddy, and comprising an extensive palette which included aubergine, blue, yellow, iron-red, translucent green, turquoise and white. These were applied in a very careful manner, particularly by one artist whose drawing of Chinese and European figures, birds and flowers was so meticulous that he has earned the title of the 'fine brush painter'. Another style features Chinese figures with particularly long, tapering hands, in landscapes, and birds with long tails.

The period between 1752 and 1756, when Dr Wall died, has

until recently been known as the 'Wall Period', but it has now been given the new name of the 'First Period'. It matters little which name is used, just as the porcelain itself is of such immeasurably greater importance than the question of whether Wall, Davis or some other as yet unidentified person was responsible for it. We have already considered some of its outstanding features as regards paste and glaze, and need only add that during the period the green translucency persisted, and that a most important feature is a thinness and neatness of potting that often serves to distinguish Worcester wares from the contemporary ones made at Caughley and Liverpool which are similarly decorated. The old test of looking for a shrinkage of glaze inside the foot-rim, leaving bare patches of unglazed paste, is by no means infallible, since other porcelains often show the same characteristic. In fact, there can be no rule-of-thumb tests of this kind when dealing with porcelains that were the subjects of continual experiment.

Many of the wares made at the time of the change-over from Bristol to Worcester were moulded ones, including a very large tureen with a dolphin knob to its cover, and jugs of various sizes formed of overlapping cabbage leaves, and, at a slightly later date, fitted with mask-shaped lips. Tea-wares were fluted, ribbed, and decorated with 'feather', 'rose and chrysanthemum' and other delicate patterns in low relief, so delicate that they can only be seen to proper advantage when a specimen is held against the light. Such wares were commonly painted in underglaze blue, mostly in the Chinese style with landscapes and figure subjects but also, perhaps a little later, in the Meissen style with flowers, flowering shrubs and insects, often complete with the crossed-swords mark. Worcester specialized in this kind of decoration, for reasons which have already been stressed. Specimens are not always marked, but those which are bear the crescent, the script W, rarely the square mark, and very often indeed one or other of a wide variety of symbols which are called 'workmen's marks', all of them in underglaze blue. The tone of the cobalt blue varies between a deep indigo and a paler colour which is often very close to the true Chinese sapphire, but we never find any traces of violet.

Outstanding among Worcester blue-painted wares are sauce-boats moulded with shell, leaf, basket-work or scrolled motifs (with moulded reserves bearing delicate Chinese landscapes and figure subjects), large hexagonal vases with domed covers, large lobed junket-dishes, openwork baskets, oval or round, with or without handles, and with applied flower-heads on the outside of the lattice-work intersections, two-handled sauce-boats, cabbage-leaf jugs with mask lips, and dainty little ovoid cream jugs with loop handles and sharply pointed lips ('sparrow-beak' jugs). Less common, and typical of the factory, we find well-moulded chamber candlesticks, caddy-spoons, egg-drainers (like caddy-spoons, but pierced, for the purpose of lifting eggs from boiling water), egg-cups, mustard-pots, little sweetmeat dishes in the forms of leaves or shells, and feeding-cups.

Although the oriental patterns, well-spaced and never too crowded, were more often pseudo-Chinese ('anglicized') in character, some of the finest seem to have been closely copied from the originals. These include the 'Hundred Antiques' (depicting a collection of articles revered by the Chinese for religious reasons), the 'Hundred Boys' (in reality a great many boys at play, but not exactly a hundred), the 'Eloping Bride' (a version of a subject featuring Chinese jugglers), the 'Prunus and Cracked Ice' (with panels of Chinese women reserved upon a blue ground, darker veined, and patterned with white prunus blossoms), and a rather crowded but nevertheless beautifully drawn concentric design of lotus flowers and leaves. No gilding was ever used on this blue-painted ware, and it is well to remember that the 'Hundred Antiques' and lotus patterns are always accompanied by their own distinctive marks. An imitation of a Chinese four- or six-character mark was usually placed upon Worcester plates and dishes decorated in powder-blue (a granulated underglaze blue obtained by blowing dry pigment through a tube, closed at one end with gauze) and bearing round and fan-shaped reserves painted with Chinese landscapes and flower-sprays. Similar plates and dishes were made at Bow, Lowestoft and Caughley, but the mark used at Worcester usually contains several camouflaged script capital Ws.

The early Chinese influence is equally apparent on the contemporary polychrome wares, of which there is bewildering variety. The simplest designs are either conventionally floral (with an occasional copy of the famille-rose, featuring large pink peonies) or else depict tall Chinese women in domestic or garden scenes. These women have been given the name of 'Long Elizas', which is a corruption of the Dutch 'Lange Liszen', or 'tall ladies'. In the same idiom, but much more elaborate, are the figures of brightly enamelled mandarins or deities, either painted on the white paste with no other ornament, or else in reserves on brocaded, gold-scrolled grounds.

Between about 1755 and 1760 the Meissen influence began to creep in, and was responsible for copies of the 'Meissen Flowers' (Meissner Blumen) in bouquets, or in the form of detached sprays. The same flowers were also rendered in light purple monochrome as an accompaniment to birds, landscapes, and flowers in ordinary enamel colours, and in crimson monochrome in much the same style as the well-known 'dry blue' painting, with gold scrolling. This peculiar, dry-looking blue enamel is in its best form peculiar to Worcester, although it was imitated at Caughley. It was used, probably by one artist only, for the painting of English garden flowers with the utmost delicacy and sureness of touch. The outlines and veining of the flowers and foliage have the appearance of having been done with a single hair, and every flower is readily recognizable. Some services were decorated with the blue alone, whereas others are further decorated with gold scrolls.

After about 1760 the Sèvres influence began to displace that of the German factory, for apart from the question of changing popular taste many Chelsea artists were leaving a factory whose days were clearly numbered. This was the period when coloured and scaled grounds began to be used, but in addition we can ascribe to it the first of a great variety of 'Japan' patterns, richly brocaded, and for the most part based upon four radiating panels of underglaze blue or 'rouge-de-fer' enamel. Other contemporary styles include copies of Kakiemon patterns, such as the 'Wheatsheaf' or the 'Banded Hedge', copies of the Chinese famille-verte, European landscapes, and good bird and flower painting.

From 1770 onwards, with the Sèvres influence predominant, the Worcester wares reached their highest peak of decorative splendour. There were of course the simpler, almost feminine festoons and arrangements of ribbons and trellises, of which the 'hop-trellis' is best known, but at the other extreme the famous 'scale' grounds are outstanding, in blue, pink, and yellow. Upon these grounds, of which by far the most common is blue, panels were reserved in which were painted, in order of rarity, figures in Watteau style, Chinese figures, 'exotic birds' and flowers. The reserves are usually beautifully outlined with gold scrolling, but in one quite common pattern, featuring Chinese flowers, its omission gives an unfinished but still quite pleasing effect. The same classes of decoration are also found reserved on plain grounds of apple-green, claret, yellow and turquoise. The exotic bird was originally of oriental origin, although this truly lovely creature reached the English decorators by way of Meissen and Sèvres. It may be seen in many different forms, painted either by factory artists or by outside decorators, all of whom rendered it in their own recognizable ways as regards shape, treatment of plumage, and background.

So much for the main decorative trends over the years of the First Period, but there are certain other aspects of the porcelain which call for mention, in particular perhaps the transferprinting technique that was used extensively from the mid-1750s. There have been many claims for the credit of using paper transfers, to which pigment was applied from engraved copper plates, for decorating porcelain, but at Worcester, at any rate, Robert Hancock and Richard Holdship began the large-scale printing on domestic wares of subjects after Pillement and others, in black, brown, red, and puce enamels. It was not long before the process was used for underglaze blue printing, and porcelain so decorated was made in enormous quantities right up to the end of the century. Indeed, such was the demand for such popular patterns as the 'pine-cone', 'medlar' and 'pheasant' that a great deal of printing was done on Worcester wares at the Caughley factory, the necessary transport being provided by the great barges known as 'Severn trows'. When a crescent mark is found on blue-printed wares it is of the hatched or shaded variety, whereas that used on painted pieces is always open. In the absence of a mark it is simple to distinguish between the free strokes of a brush, and brush-made, washed-in shading, and the more mechanical hatched shading and rigid drawing necessitated by the use of the engraver's tools.

The best known of all black overglaze transferred prints is the 'Tea Party', although the famous 'King of Prussia' pattern is almost as common. There is something very attractive about them, although many collectors prefer the less accomplished, earlier little vignettes of sailing-ships, swans and squirrels, and the equally delicate Chinese subjects. In this regard, a word of warning to the beginner who may at first sight confuse a black-printed specimen with one decorated in a superficially similar, but in reality quite a different way. This is by delicate brush 'pencilling' in black enamel, usually featuring Chinese figures and landscapes, but occasionally flowers and butterflies. This kind of decoration, which is also rarely found on Longton Hall wares, was practised during the period about 1760–5.

Many customers who ordered Chinese services had their armorial bearings painted on them, and they naturally continued the practice when they bought an English substitute. The very early examples of this 'armorial' porcelain which was made at Worcester, from 1755 onwards, bear rococo shields set in softly painted landscapes, but after about 1760 the shields are more usually painted directly on the white body of the ware, accompanied by foliate designs and scattered flower-sprigs, in polychrome or in purple monochrome. Towards the end of the 1760s use was sometimes made of a black-transferred shield, which was then filled in with enamels to any desired scheme.

Though the factory obviously had a large staff of skilled

decorators, a great deal of work was nevertheless painted in outside decorating studios, mostly with birds, flowers, fruit and figure subjects. Some very splendid though rather crowded figure subjects on important vases and other decorative wares were painted by John Donaldson; and O'Neale, the Chelsea 'fable painter', applied his animal and fable subjects to a great deal of Worcester also. Pieces painted by these two artists are naturally very rare, but the brushwork of decorators employed by James

Figure 6. 'Black pencilling' on Worcester porcelain.

Giles, in London, is quite often found, and includes a rendering of the exotic birds whose frightened, ruffled appearance well merits the description of 'dishevelled bird'; flower-painting in very bright colours, featuring very large bouquets and sprays of English garden flowers, the painting of large flowers and extremely large moths, nearly four inches across their wings, in very crude but colourful enamels, and the work of the 'spotted fruit painter' which usually includes a sliced pear, often a vegetable or two and, of course, some 'spotted' fruits. Apparently Giles bought Worcester porcelain in the white for this purpose, but he bought also a great deal of porcelain already black-transferred, to which he added enamels and gilding, often with very attractive effect.

Though Wall died in 1776 the First Period did not really end until Davis died in 1783. The London agent, Thomas Flight, then bought the business for his sons, Joseph and John. So began the so-called Flight Period, though in fact there were several changes in partnership between 1783 and 1840, when amalgamation was made with the rival Chamberlain company. Thus, in 1793 the firm was Flight & Barr (Thomas Barr), in 1807 Barr, Flight & Barr, and in 1813 Flight, Barr & Barr.

For some time the old styles were for the most part continued, and the old crescent mark, though much smaller in size, was retained. The steatite paste was, however, discarded in favour of variations of the Spode bone-ash body, which was very durable, whiter, and more translucent. Variations, because experiment never ceased, as we may see from Martin Barr's very hard, greyish paste which was often marked with an incised B, and the several ones of exceptionally fine quality which probably resulted from the employment, for a short time, of William Billingsley. He was not allowed to make his own expensive Swansea and Nantgarw pastes, but much porcelain of the period is almost equal to them, The old, soft honey-gilding was replaced by a new, brassier, gaudier variety applied by means of a gold-mercury amalgam.

Some of the more splendid Flight wares were made for Royalty, the nobility and the great London companies, mostly in what may be called the Empire style, with lavish use of splendid gold in every kind of design, matt and burnished, flat and raised. Classical shapes, many in the Sèvres style, were used for vases and other ornamental wares, with handles modelled after the human figure, snakes and animals, or intricately scrolled. There was a great deal of 'jewelling' with little porcelain globules round rims, necks and bases. The better wares were painted by such proficient known artists as James Pennington, who is known for his figures of Hope, by the sea-shore in various poses, on a service made for the Duke of Clarence. Thomas Baxter and John Barker painted shells in a detailed, lifelike manner, exotic birds were still painted in the old style by George Davis, and

there were others equally gifted but unknown. The most characteristic of the domestic wares were spirally fluted, and decorated
with slight sprig patterns in black, blue, puce, brown or pink,
with or without wide, dark underglaze blue borders gilded in
foliate or geometrical patterns. Underglaze blue was still used,
usually with gilding, though some patterns, such as the lotus-
based 'Queen Charlotte', were sometimes left without it.

The rival factory of Chamberlains was founded in 1786 when
Robert and his brother Humphrey, both painters, left Flights
to found what was at first a decorating studio, dealing mainly
with white wares bought from Turner at Caughley. It was not
long before the new company made its own porcelain, which was
at first rather heavy, grey, with a rippled surface to the glaze and
a yellowish-brown translucency. As at Flights, however, the
paste was always experimental, until in 1795 the fine 'Regent'
body was perfected. This is extremely white and translucent, and
it was apparently reserved for the making of important services
and the best decorative wares.

There is very little difference between the decoration found on
Flights and Chamberlains porcelain, and indeed many artists of
note worked at both factories at various times. Humphrey
Chamberlain himself painted scenes from 'Paradise Lost' in a
palette of pale pastel colours, in a style intended to avoid showing any brushmarks. The flower-painting, like that seen upon
Flight wares, was done in the naturalistic Derby tradition, and
many fine services were made, notably those in armorial style,
often with an extravagant use of Japan patterns. Many of the
landscapes take the form of views of Malvern or Worcester, and
an occasional one of Cheltenham reminds us that even the great
Worcester factories still owed a great deal to the patronage of
Society. The landscapes and the flower-painting are usually
reserved upon good ground colours which include a strong claret
and a characteristic matt cobalt-blue, and we find a prolific use
of gilding in the form of foliate scrolling.

It is perhaps not widely known that a number of figures was
made at the Chamberlain factory, including sheep and dogs

(often on bases painted with the matt cobalt-blue), boys in short jackets and pantaloons, girls in sprigged crinolines, and a rare set known as the 'Tyrolean Singers'. A small number of finely modelled cottage pastille-burners was also produced, though in the usual absence of a factory mark they are very difficult to distinguish from those made at Coalport, Rockingham, and in Staffordshire. The Chamberlain proprietorship passed in 1852 to Kerr & Binns and, finally, in 1862, the present Royal Worcester Porcelain Company was formed.

Mention must be made of yet a third offshoot of the original Worcester concern, which was founded in 1800 by Thomas Grainger, a nephew of Humphrey Chamberlain, and which was amalgamated with the present company in 1888. Decoration of the white, translucent bone-ash porcelain naturally differs very little from that which is found upon the wares of the two larger factories, but a characteristic feature of some careful but rather 'pretty' flower-painting is the presence of pale pink harebells. It is fortunate that most Grainger ware, in common with that of the Flights and the Chamberlains, bears factory marks. It is noteworthy, however, that it was the custom of all three factories to mark but a few pieces of a large service.

CHAPTER FIVE

Caughley and Coalport porcelain

SALOPIAN porcelain, as it is often called, was made at Caughley (pronounced Calfley) from 1772, and at nearby Coalport from 1814 until the works finally closed some years ago. The first proprietor was Thomas Turner, son-in-law of a Mr Gallimore, who had been making earthenware for about twenty years on the same spot.

Caughley porcelain is sometimes referred to as the 'poor man's Worcester', and indeed the blue-printed wares that made up most of the factory's very considerable output are very like those made

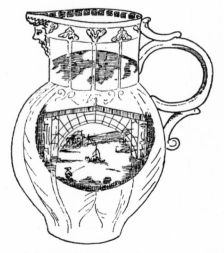

Figure 7. A blue-printed jug of Caughley porcelain.

at Worcester, though the steatitic paste has a brownish trans-lucency because the glaze was not blued with cobalt. The glaze itself never has the unmistakable glistening quality of that used at Worcester, being sometimes almost matt, and often rather pitted. If these factors are not enough to enable the collector to identify the ware, then he looks for foot-rims which are commonly rectangular in section, instead of bluntly triangular as on Worcester specimens, and for a noticeable comparative clumsiness in much of the potting.

It is important to recognize the fact that when public demand made it necessary a great deal of printing on Worcester porcelain was done at Caughley. This accounts for the presence of the Salopian S mark on many specimens which must, on the evidence of paste and potting, be attributed to Worcester and, sometimes, for the violet tone of the underglaze blue. This characteristic colour, which was never used at Worcester, was introduced by Turner after a visit which he paid to the French factories, but on the other hand much of the Caughley blue printing and painting is of quite normal tone. Turner was himself an engraver who had learnt his trade under Hancock, and his prints have a peculiar appearance of having been drawn with a ruler in parallel, equally spaced lines as regards the rendering of water and shading. Compared with Worcester work they are characteristically mechanical and formal. Thomas Minton, the founder of the great pottery in Stoke which bears his name, was a pupil of Turner, and among his designs on Caughley wares are the 'Broseley Dragon' and the 'Willow Pattern'. It is interesting to remember that the latter had no Chinese counterpart, being merely a crowded arrangement of many Chinese motifs, and that the famous legend was invented merely to popularize the pattern. Later on, probably in an attempt to retain a market which was fast being lost as a result of English enterprise, the Chinese exported wares which they laboriously painted with the same pattern. Other Caughley patterns printed in underglaze blue are the 'Fisherman', the 'Pheasant' and the 'Cornflower', and whereas Worcester blue and white invariably has borders in the Chinese style, a single blue line, or no border at all, it is usual on Caughley pieces to find elaborate brocaded borders, often interrupted by small scrolled reserves containing landscapes or farmyard animals.

Blue painting is not often found on Caughley porcelain, possibly because by the time the factory was in full production the quicker, cheaper method of printing was fully developed throughout the industry. Nevertheless, some was done, notably of the 'Cornflower' pattern, but also in the forms of flower sprays and 'Long Elizas'. Powder-blue plates were produced, exactly similar to those made at Worcester, Lowestoft and Bow, but peculiar to Caughley is a design featuring alternate radiating panels of powder-blue and Chinese emblems, the centre containing a flowering shrub.

The Caughley management rarely attempted to rival Worcester as regards enamelled decoration, although it is clear that they had at their command some very fine colours, in particular a very clear yellow and some good, translucent greens. On domestic wares we find flower-painting in the form of closely packed bouquets, often with brown leaves veined in gold, and pink roses shaded in darker red, in the style of Lowestoft and of Chinese 'export' wares. Lowestoft was probably the source also of the rather crude fish-scale borders in pink or red, and the Worcester 'dry blue' was copied with indifferent success. Some of the fluted wares, decorated with simple sprig patterns, are very like those painted at Chamberlains. The Caughley gold is of good quality, but it must be remembered that much of the gilding on blue and white ware was applied by outside decorators. On the other hand, the factory gilders were probably responsible for the all-gold patterns which show to fine advantage on the creamy paste.

The Caughley factory was purchased in 1799 by John Rose, a former apprentice of Turner, and in 1814 he moved everything across the river to the factory at Coalport which he already owned. Blue and white was still made for a few years, but otherwise the emphasis was always thereafter on splendour and, multiplicity of coloured styles. The Coalport paste and glaze is uniformly fine, and whitely translucent, especially after Billingsley joined the factory staff in 1820. It is doubtful whether he was engaged as chemist or decorator, but although it is improbable that he was permitted to introduce his own expensive paste, there is no doubt that under his guidance the Coalport body very nearly approached it in excellence. In this regard, it is interesting, and perhaps significant, to remember that copper plates engraved with the word SWANSEA were still in the possession of the Coalport concern until a few years ago.

Between about 1820 and the middle of the century, then, a very fine porcelain was made which is often mistaken for the more valuable Nantgarw and Swansea. Certain large jugs, in particular, painted with flowers which include large roses in what is mistakenly called the 'Billingsley style', and a very large class of single- and double-handled mugs similarly decorated but often bearing initials, dates and scrolling in gold, are of particularly fine quality. The Coalport pattern books, which still exist, show that the Coalport designers produced a great number of gaudy Japan patterns in red, green, blue, and gold, but for the most part the emphasis was on the Sèvres taste, with festoons and swags of flowers, urns, and many scrolled borders. Some fine bird-painting was done, also in the Sèvres (and Chelsea) style, notably by two painters named John Randall and Mottershead. The birds are of the 'exotic' type, with long legs, painted in blue, bright yellow, puce, and brick-red, and though pieces so decorated were originally marked with an anchor and a letter C in blue, we sometimes find that these authentic marks have been removed by acid, to be replaced by a misleading small gold anchor. There is a great variety of first-class coloured grounds, including maroon, celeste (turquoise), celadon green, canary, apple-green, 'venus pink' (Rose Pompadour), buff, blue, brown, and pink. The domestic wares of the period are almost impossible to distinguish from those made at Worcester, Derby, Longport and elsewhere in the Potteries, but mention should be made of a class of toilet-ware, jugs, and dinner- and tea-ware which is always ascribed to the factory. It is easily identified by all-over moulding of flowers in low relief, accompanied by bold painting of English garden flowers.

The 'raised flower' pieces of this period are usually given the name of 'Coalbrookdale', a fact which has given rise to the theory that they were made at quite a different factory. It must be admitted that there is reason to believe that there was more than one factory in existence at the beginning of the century, but it has been found impossible to find out anything about it, and there is really no reason to think that this class of ware was made any-

Figure 8. 'Coalbrookdale' vase with applied flowers.

where but at Rose's own factory. The applied flowers and leaves are always beautifully modelled and coloured, though at times applied so lavishly as to obscure the lines and the surface nature of the porcelain. The earlier pieces are distinguished by more careful modelling, and by the use of a distinctive yellow-green, picked out in gold, for the rococo type of handle which was always used. On the whole, it is safe to say that the sets of very large vases, with covers, are comparatively late.

Most of the 'Coalbrookdale ware' is unmarked, and it is not

easy to distinguish it from the very similar ware made at Derby, Rockingham and Worcester (Chamberlains), particularly as each factory used the same device of painting a landscape on the one side and a bouquet of flowers on the other, of a vase or other ornamental piece. One can only expect to find a Bloor period mark on a piece of Derby, and to recognize the coppery gilding and general heaviness and exuberance of Rockingham. On the other hand, the application of coloured applied flowers to a dark mazarine-blue ground is peculiar to Coalport.

To many connoisseurs the finest Coalport is that which was made from about 1850 onwards, when Rose succeeded in improving his coloured grounds, notably the Bleu-de-Roi, Turquoise and Rose Pompadour, to such an extent that his wares were equal to the finest Sèvres. In fact, it is recorded that in answer to the demand of the London dealers the Sèvres mark was actually applied to some of the ware. Practically every old Sèvres form and decorative style was copied, with landscapes, trophies of war, birds, flowers and idyllic conversation pieces in the Watteau style painted in reserves on the coloured grounds, lavishly gilded. At the same time, however, many of the table wares of the period were soberly designed, including tea-sets plain white and with wide, shallow, spiral flutes, the handles sometimes gilded, and services of all kinds decorated with the popular Coalport 'Indian Tree' pattern.

An important class of ware which properly falls into the scope of this chapter was made by Thomas Martin Randall, a Caughley apprentice and London outside decorator, who set up kilns at Madeley, near Coalport, about 1825. Since he is said to have worked with Billingsley at Pinxton it is to be expected that his porcelain is of remarkably fine quality. Like Rose, he decorated his ware in the Sèvres style, but unlike him he always refused to add the Sèvres mark. Some fine bird painting was done by his nephew, John, who as we have seen painted also at Coalport. Robert Bix Gray painted flowers and fruit, birds and portraits, and Phillip Ballard painted pastoral scenes in the Watteau style. Lithophanes were made, both white and coloured. In these pieces, which were imitations of the similar ones made first at Berlin (though of course in true porcelain), the effect was obtained by means of the varying thicknesses of the moulded slabs of porcelain, which were intended for use as lamp-shade panels and so forth.

CHAPTER SIX

Derby porcelain

WILLIAM DUESBURY was a practical businessman whose aim was to produce sensible but well-decorated porcelain for everybody. He was not dependent upon any kind of patronage, and he did not lay himself out to cater for the gentry and nobility. His partners in the venture, the beginnings of which in the early 1750s are somewhat obscure, were John Heath and Andrew Planché, and such was their success that they were able to absorb the factories of Chelsea, Bow and Longton Hall, on each occasion making the most of whatever merit the wares of each could afford. After Duesbury died, in 1786, his son and Robert Bloor found difficulty in keeping up his high standards, and though much good ware was still made it was seldom as artistic, and the factory closed down in 1848. That was not the end of porcelain making in Derby, however, for almost immediately the business was taken over by Bloor's clerk, William Locker, and removed from the Nottingham Road to King Street. Later proprietors in this venture were Stevenson and Hancock, whose ware, including figures, was made in most of the old styles. The wares of both these factories should properly be called Derby, whereas 'Royal Crown Derby' was made at yet a third factory, founded in 1877 and situated in the Osmaston Road, in competition with the King Street company. The third factory is still flourishing.

The earliest identifiable porcelain made at Derby is glassy and chalky white, very thinly glazed, very clean and free from blemish, with a pale yellow translucency. Very little blue-painting was attempted until the Chelsea-Derby years (1770–84), but there were several early polychrome styles. One painter's work can be recognized by his unusually large moths and other insects, copied from Meissen, and by birds and landscapes which show the same mannerisms. Yet another painted flowers with very

53

thin stalks. A dirty turquoise enamel and a particularly dark *gros-bleu* ground are characteristic of the period.

With the taking over of the Chelsea factory in 1770 began the most splendid era of Derby decoration on domestic wares, about which much has been said in a previous chapter. With the aid of artists and chemists who left London to join him in Derby, Duesbury was able to take the best of the Sèvres-Chelsea styles, and to produce Derby patterns which set a standard for all the English factories with the possible exception of Worcester, even

Figure 9. A typical mug form made at Derby.

though his commercial instinct sometimes led him to allow them to become somewhat mechanical in appearance. We find ground colours of claret and turquoise which are not quite of Chelsea excellence, and the appearance of a lapis-lazuli blue, known to the collector as 'Derby Blue' which replaced the dark mazarine. There is a profusion of festoons and swags, scattered detached flower-sprays, attractive painting of urns and classical figures in grey or crimson monochrome, and a variety of striped and wavy patterns of which the 'gold stripes', with or without flowers, is best known. Many designs were copied from Worcester, including one of simple black and grey husks, some Japans, and a version of the spirally-radiating 'whorl' pattern in blue, red and gold. The underglaze blue-painting is very good indeed, though it was confined to a few patterns, the most common of which features a very simple Chinese landscape within a shaded key-pattern border.

During the period 1784 to about 1810, when the well-known crown-and-crossed-batons mark was used, many specialist artists worked upon services and upon cabinet pieces such as coffee-cans, painted in almost miniature style, and bearing good ground colours of yellow, pale red, fawn, pink, claret and turquoise.

Figure 10. A blue-painted pattern on Derby porcelain.

They worked upon a still excellent paste, white and translucent, which unfortunately had a tendency towards crazing which often mars the appearance of the finest specimens. It was once thought that the identity of Derby artists could be ascertained by the presence of numbers upon the ware, but since there is considerable difference of opinion as to their true significance the collector relies more upon style of painting in this regard. The flowers of William ('Quaker') Pegg can be identified by virtue of their large size, their fidelity to nature, and by his habit of writing the names of the blossoms upon the backs of every piece. Billingsley's flowers on Derby, as indeed on any other kind of porcelain, are very seldom seen, but once seen and studied his typical wiped-out highlights cannot be mistaken. Edward Withers, the earliest known of all Derby artists, had a style in which the petals of each flower were conventionally outlined, and another Chelsea painter, Richard Askew, is famous for his cupids in crimson and grey. John Brewer made a speciality of sea-scapes and shipping, and both he and his brother Robert shared with Zachariah Boreman (1783–94) and 'Jockey' Hill the responsibility for very fine landscape painting. Boreman drew his details in monochrome, afterwards filling them in with subdued colours, whereas Hill's predominating greens and yellows are much stronger.

The general opinion is that Bloor's managership brought with it a gradual and general artistic decline, and that financial difficulties enforced the sale of 'seconds' that had been put aside during the preceding period. It is certain, at least, that the cheaper Staffordshire bone-ash paste was adopted. Nevertheless, much that is good was made during the period, even though a great deal of the decoration was but mediocre by Derby standards. Flower-painting, for instance, was no longer individual and distinctive, for the new conventional style, probably introduced by Edwin and Horatio Steele, was common throughout the Potteries, and at Coalport and Rockingham, featuring hard drawing and a palette of colours which always favoured deep orange, brownish red, and raw pink. One exception to this general rule, perhaps, was the work of Moses Webster, who clung to the old tradition and whose roses in particular are always naturally rendered. Another style of decoration, very common on the later Worcester wares, and very like oil-painting, was carried out at Derby by William Corden.

The figures made at Derby, many of them from Chelsea moulds or at least in the Chelsea style, are frequently mistaken for Chelsea or Bow. Nevertheless, there are many distinguishing features. The models made between about 1755 and 1770 almost always have three or four darker, unglazed patches caused by the pads of clay upon which they rested in the kiln. Furthermore, these 'patch marks' pieces usually have hectic red patches on their cheeks, and their colouring often includes a brownish turquoise-green. Other guides to identification are a narrow band (or 'dry edge') of unglazed paste beneath the foot, a glaze which is milky with no trace of the Bow greenish glaze, and great restraint in the brocading of women's dresses. Towards the end of the century there was a tendency towards showiness, with lavish use of brassy gilding but much less careful modelling. A notable exception to this lapse was the production, during the later Crown Derby period, of white biscuit figures, the best of which were modelled by John James Spengler and Pierre Stephan. At best, and before Bloor took over, the biscuit body was as smooth as ivory, almost greasy, with a very slight, accidental film of glaze which did not, of course, detract from the sharpness of the modelling.

The collector should beware of two pitfalls where Derby figures are concerned. There are on the market many specimens, some of them of large size, which were made by the notorious Samson of Paris, complete with prominent, much too boldly drawn marks. They are superficially very like the true Derby, but their hard-paste body is readily apparent, especially under the base. Other figures, replicas and not forgeries, were made at Derby by Stevenson and Hancock between 1850 and 1870. Their later origin is betrayed by the presence of the letters S and H on either side of the crown-and-crossed-batons mark.

CHAPTER SEVEN

Longton Hall porcelain

THE short-lived factory founded about 1750 at Longton Hall and popularly associated with the name of William Littler had the distinction of being, as far as we know, the only pioneer porcelain-making concern to be situated in the Potteries, long acknowledged as the centre of potting in this country. Until quite recently many of the wares that were made during the ten-year span of the factory's life were credited to others, if credited is indeed the word, for it must be admitted that many of them are more interesting than beautiful. Mr Bernard Watney has conducted site excavations which, with various contemporary documents unearthed by him and by others, have afforded much valuable information as regards paste constitution and decoration. The result is that though much research still remains to be done it is now possible to identify a considerable range of Longton Hall ware. It should be stressed at this point, however, that there is documentary evidence which seems to indicate that it was actually one of Littler's partners, William Jenkinson, who had discovered a way of making porcelain, though since he had no experience of practical potting it was natural that he should enlist the aid of someone who had, he himself withdrawing from the venture shortly afterwards, in August 1753. Littler was an experienced maker of salt-glazed earthenware, and the inventor of a remarkable opaque blue enamel which we now call 'Littler's Blue', but though he was able to obtain financial assistance from various sources he was forced to abandon the undertaking in 1760, and in fact died a poor man in 1784.

Dealing first with the wares made during Jenkinson's activity, we find that the domestic wares were moulded with scrolled or floral reserves, basketwork, flutes and ribs, fruit, flowers and leaves. In fact, in silver shapes and in the styles of the salt-glazed wares which had copied them, and with which Littler was familiar. The paste is glassy and very like that used at Chelsea, with a translucency varying between strong green and cloudy yellows, and sometimes showing 'moons'. The potting was invariably heavy and clumsy, and fire-cracks and warping are common-place. Beneath the bases, which often had to be ground flat, the glaze has collected in bluish blobs, like candle-fat.

Some of the many overlapping leaf forms of these early domestic wares, the sauce-boats, pickle-trays and so on, are well-nigh covered with Littler's vivid, mottled blue, though it must be remembered that the unfired size-gilding which origin-ally embellished borders and picked out moulded reserves, and which, of course, somewhat relieved the intense colour, has usually long-since vanished. An alternative to the gilding, less commonly used, was raised white enamel. The enamels used in the decoration of the early polychrome wares are soft and pastel-like. There is some good flower painting, well-drawn and well-spaced; bird painting, oriental quail and orange-banded pat-terns, and an occasional *tour de force* such as the Watteau-like scene reserved upon a Littler's Blue ground, with white-enamel scrolling, on a large coffee-pot in the V. and A. Museum.

Figures were made from the very beginning, and the earliest belong to a group which has been given the descriptive name of 'snow-man'. Over thirty different models have been identified, all of them very reminiscent, as regards style, of contemporary ones made at Meissen and Chelsea, though the modelling is so poor that it suggests the difficulty that must have been encoun-tered in manipulating such a 'short', non-coherent paste. Most are hollow, their bases unglazed and pierced with small conical holes, while in places the thick, glassy glaze has either failed to adhere to the paste, or else has collected in blobs.

After Jenkinson's departure, and until about 1757, the wares greatly improved both from the technical and the artistic aspects. Domestic wares became more elegant, with more intricate moulding, of strawberries and leaf forms, with an occasional openwork rim. Cups are usually tall and narrow, circular or hexagonal in section, and a typical Longton handle is of a double scroll type difficult to describe but easily recognizable when once seen. The colours became brighter, with the introduction of bright purplish-pink, good orange-red, opaque blue, and bluish and yellowish greens. The pink and yellowish green are commonly seen in conjunction when used for the outlining and veining of moulded leaf patterns. Technically very much in the Worcester style, but quite different in appearance, are specimens pencilled in black, and washed in with thin enamels. Among the

Figure 11. A moulded leaf pattern typical of Longton Hall.

many pieces which show Chinese influence are those painted rather sketchily in underglaze blue.

The Longton figures of the middle period are a great advance on the earlier ones, often being equal as far as detailed modelling is concerned, to those made at Chelsea, but usually decorated with exceedingly bright, strong enamels. A thick brown, a very strong pink, dark blue, and yellowish green comprise the most usual colour arrangement, and the cheeks of faces, as at Derby, were often reddened. The paste of which these and the domestic wares were made has a strong green translucency, often containing 'moons' or little flecks of greater translucency. The soft, easily scratched glaze has a silky feel and a wet-looking, glistening appearance. A common feature is that it has run, carrying underglaze blue with it, in streaks and lines.

The last three years of the factory were years of struggle, during which Littler strove to keep his head above water by the production of useful domestic wares, most of them decorated in underglaze blue. These included coffee, chocolate and tea sets, and the familiar reeded cylindrical mugs with moulded

Figure 12. Moulding and 'Littler's Blue' on a Longton Hall mug.

scrolled reserves on either side, and double-scrolled handles. No other kind of ware could be made so cheaply, for as far as we know printing was not attempted at Longton Hall, although there is reason to believe that Sadler of Liverpool bought Longton ware which he decorated with his usual black-printed designs. Figures were not neglected, since they too were in great popular demand, and some large ones were made, up to over sixteen inches in height, painted in the same strong colours as before. The modelling will stand comparison with that of any contemporary English factory, and well-known models include some spirited horses after Meissen originals, a wonderful mounted Duke of Brunswick, and a set of 'Continents' very like those made at Plymouth.

The end of a courageous venture, and a successful one in many ways, came when in September 1760 no less than 'upwards of ninety thousand pieces' were sold by auction in Salisbury. If some of them were unfinished, as seems most likely, we have a plausible explanation of the fact that many a piece which would otherwise pass as Longton Hall is rejected by the collector because the decoration upon it is not typical of the factory.

CHAPTER EIGHT

Liverpool porcelain

SINCE the port of Liverpool was one of the delft-making centres of the mid-eighteenth century it would have been strange if its potters had not tried to make the new kind of ware which was threatening their livelihood. In fact, between 1755 and about 1770 about a dozen of them are known to have begun to make porcelain, though according to contemporary documentary evidence their businesses began to decline by the mid 1770s, probably because the Staffordshire competition, led by Wedgwood, proved too strong to be resisted.

For some time past the name Liverpool has been conveniently given to porcelain which could not easily be attributed to any of the well-known factories, or which was 'not quite good enough for Worcester'. At the other extreme, some writers, often convincingly and with good reason, have of late credited the Liverpool men with the making of a great deal of ware which is of such superior quality, or of such design, that it has always been attributed to other manufactories. It is perhaps best here to steer a middle course, and to describe those characteristic wares about which there can be little doubt.

The first porcelain maker in Liverpool, of whom we have firm knowledge, was Robert Podmore, a potter from the Worcester works, who in 1755 entered into an agreement with Richard Chaffers and Philip Christian. He was to supply the knowledge, and his partners the capital. It is clear, judging by all available evidence, that the firm set the standard of porcelain making in Liverpool, which indeed would be expected, bearing in mind Podmore's training. The others who opened up within a short space of time were Reid & Co., Samuel Gilbody, William Ball, Zachariah Barnes & Cotter, James & John Pennington, and Seth Pennington.

When Podmore joined Chaffers he brought with him not only the formula of a workable steatite body, but also the early Worcester custom of basing decoration upon Chinese styles. Although each of the potters listed above had his own establishment, it was natural that they followed Podmore's lead in both regards, and it is a fact that with understandable exceptions, as

Figure 13. A 'biting snake' handle typical of Liverpool porcelain.

they found their own feet, they made wares which have very similar characteristics.

Dealing first with the porcelain made during what is usually known as the Chaffers period, that is from 1755 until he died ten years later, we naturally find a ware very like that made at Worcester, since Podmore understood no other. The potting is thin and neat, the paste has a green translucency, and the glaze is thin, glistening, bluish green in colour, and has not always 'taken' inside the foot-rim. Shapes and mouldings, again, approximate to those used at Worcester, but an important difference concerns the foot-rims of cups, saucers and bowls, which slope inwards so as to merit the description of 'undercut'. Another Liverpool characteristic is a handle the upper terminal of which is either cloven, or shaped like a snake's head, to grip the rim of the vessel.

What happened to Podmore after Chaffer's death we do not know, and Christian appears to have been something of a sleeping partner. At any rate, the ware began to change as soapstone was gradually discarded, to be replaced by bone-ash. The result was a bluish white body instead of one which always inclined to grey, with usually a yellowish translucency. The glaze is of a dirty bluish colour, and it tends to collect with a characteristic 'thunder-cloud' effect behind foot-rims. The undercut foot-rims of the earlier period are replaced by wedge-shaped ones, and more ambitious moulding was attempted. Among the new forms in this regard is a tea-pot formerly attributed to Longton Hall, with moulded palm trees rising from a row of leaves around the base. Sauce-boats are usually of silver shape, the best known featuring three moulded arched panels on either side, resting upon a row of acanthus leaves. The helmet shape was preferred for cream jugs. In general, and as we might expect, this period between 1765 and about 1780 was one during which teething troubles were overcome, with an end to warping, fire-cracks, and misshapen foot-rims.

Between 1780 and the end of the century, when Seth Pennington seems to have been the leading spirit in the Liverpool industry, the bone-ash body was supreme, and though it and the improved, clearer glaze upon it show a perfected technique, the advance upon earlier wares shows itself more in decoration than in potting. In fact, it is now time to consider the whole question of Liverpool decoration, dealing first with the blue and white which was made throughout every period.

At first the blue-painted designs were direct copies of the Worcester ones, though there are one or two exceptions. A design found on no other ware features a slender, double-trunked palm tree standing before a fence which disappears on the right behind what seem to be five upright boards surmounted by a peony. This design, like so many others painted at Liverpool, has a simple trellis border. After about 1765 a much greater variety of original patterns was evolved, one of the few late ones still owing its origin to Worcester being a variety of what Dr Boney has aptly termed the 'peg-top and ramp' design, a water scene featuring the central 'peg-top' (whatever it was

Figure 14. Liverpool saucer painted in underglaze blue with 'peg-top and ramp' pattern.

meant to represent) between two gnarled trees and a pavilion with, again, the trellis border. There is a wide variety of floral patterns with petals half filled in with blue, and solid fern-like leaves, one of which features foliate sprays interrupted by what seem to be daisies, with solid blue centres. The 'Jumping Boy' pattern of Bow was a Liverpool favourite. Above all, there is a wide variety of moulded cups and saucers, sauce-boats and jugs with blue-painted Chinese vignettes, or with one or other of the many blue-painted diaper, trellis or cell borders.

There is little that can be said about Liverpool blue-printing, which probably began between 1765 and 1769. Much of it was done in a very heavy, wet-looking dark blue that cannot be compared technically with the clear-cut Worcester work. A design of a Chinese woman and child in a garden, enclosed within an elaborate, deep scrolled diaper and foliate border was clearly copied from a Caughley pattern. The original kind of printing, in black, is not so common on Liverpool wares as one might expect, considering that Sadler had his works in the city. It is probable that he was fully occupied in dealing with cream-ware. Nevertheless, there are a number of patterns printed in black, sepia, brown, purple and red, including the 'Tea Party', 'King of Prussia', 'Ruins', 'Parrot and Fruit' and 'William Pitt', while a black outline washed in with enamels was used for the Liverpool version of the Worcester 'red cow' design. Mention must also be made of a class of ware now ascribed to Sadler, and so to Liverpool porcelain, decorated with different enamels cleverly applied by means of a single transfer.

Polychrome decoration, whether applied inside the factories or by outside decorators, is on the whole unpretentious, with a sparing use of gold. Many of the blue-painted patterns were 'improved' by means of red enamelling, with much of the detail outlined in gold. We find the typical Chinese landscapes, the Chinese figures in garden scenes (including a pattern featuring a lady with an umbrella, and a Chinaman beckoning to her—the 'beckoning Chinaman'), a number of Japan patterns distinguished from the Worcester versions by their streaky blue bands, and a few Kakiemon designs such as the 'banded hedge'. Some English flower-painting in the naturalistic style was attempted, probably on very late wares.

A feature of the finest porcelains made at most other factories, ground colours, is not often to be found on Liverpool ware. The blue was so uneven and streaky that when used it was usually 'marbled' or trellissed in gold, and the scaled grounds used at Worcester demanded too many working hours to allow of their use. It is perhaps a fair summing-up to say that Liverpool decoration was just as good as it had to be if the wares were to be sold, but that very occasionally we may expect to find a specimen so elaborately painted, well drawn, in good strong enamels and profusely gilded, as to show what might have been but for outside competition.

CHAPTER NINE

Lowestoft porcelain

THE porcelain made at Lowestoft between 1760 and 1802 has no connexion whatever with the so-called 'Chinese Lowestoft' with its characteristic 'hard', grey paste, plaited handles, heraldry, pink roses and applied white-clay ornament. The latter is a Chinese ware that was made for export (and incidentally much copied by Samson of Paris), whereas true Lowestoft is essentially English, simple in design and in decoration, and made in a small factory the proprietors of which had no desire to emulate either the Chinese wares or the ambitious splendour of their rivals in this country. Indeed, the standard is set for us, perhaps, by the dainty little dolls' tea-sets made at Lowestoft, so that the word 'toy-like' is a singularly apt description.

In 1757 Robert Browne, a chemist, founded a small company which within a few years was making a creamy, bone-ash porcelain covered with a thin, blue-tinted glaze which tended to run, taking underglaze blue with it. Translucency is commonly quite colourless, but occasionally palely green, and a constant feature of tea-bowls, cups and slop-bowls is a shallow sagging, almost to a point, within the foot-rim.

In common with other factories the early ware was almost entirely decorated in underglaze blue, and when Worcester designs were copied it was common practice to copy also the marks of the crescent or the Meissen crossed swords. These marks were drawn on a very small scale, in keeping with the unusually small size of pieces of domestic ware. The average diameter of a tea-bowl, for instance, is about three inches. Coffee-cups are rare, possibly because the typical loop-handled tea-cup was meant to serve both beverages. Lowestoft tea-pots are usually globular, usually with closed rose-bud knobs to their covers, and with the undersides of the cover flanges glazed. Coffee-pots are of the graceful Worcester shape, with scrolled handles, high-domed covers, and unusually large spouts. The Lowestoft tea-caddy, an indispensable part of every tea-service, was made not in the Worcester ovoid shape, but rectangular, small, in the 'Chinese Lowestoft' style. Other common forms include octagonal ink-pots, feeding-cups, egg-cups and eye-baths. Many wares were moulded, and peculiar to the factory is a design of three radial bands of trellis pattern, and circular medallions, which sometimes incorporates the moulded initials IH and the date 1764. From Worcester was copied the sauce-boat (or butter-boat) in the shape of a nautilus shell, and several

Figure 15. Moulded and blue-printed Lowestoft.

larger ones, some up to nine inches in length, with moulded reserves on either side. A Lowestoft variant of the Worcester 'mask-lip' jug has a moulded all-over floral pattern upon which is painted a Chinese landscape, in underglaze blue, and a lip on which the features are very crudely drawn.

Lowestoft underglaze blue is almost indigo in tone, and its curiously granulated appearance is best seen on a pattern of radiating spirals of scale-blue, alternating with panels of simple flower-painting, Scale-blue is not found in any other form on Lowestoft porcelain. Powder-blue of a mazarine-like depth, and attractively uneven, was used in two ways, however, with a central reserve surrounded by irregularly-shaped ones containing views of Lowestoft, or more commonly in the manner of Bow, with fan-shaped reserves. The bulk of the blue-painted designs were copied from those used at the latter factory and at Worcester, mostly Chinese landscapes and simple arrangements of flowers, flowering shrubs and rock-like masses. From Berlin and Copenhagen came the simple 'Immortelle' or 'Copenhagen' arrangement of flower-sprays, and direct from a Chinese original an attractive arrangement of flowers centring around a peony. This particular pattern is often drawn so clearly and attractively that it compares very favourably with the best that Worcester

Figure 16. Typical blue painting on a Lowestoft saucer.

could do. A noteworthy distinguishing feature of many jugs and mugs is the presence on either side of the handle terminals, in the Chinese style, of a short blue line.

A word should be said concerning the marks on Lowestoft blue-painted wares. Whereas at Worcester workmen's marks were used as alternatives to the factory marks, and at Bow the artists' numerals were placed usually fairly near the centres of bases, the Lowestoft numerals, commonly ranging between 1 and 30, are found close to the foot-rims.

Blue-printing of comparatively poor quality was done after

about 1770, and the comparative lack of skill of the Lowestoft engravers is indicated by a marked hesitancy, almost a trembling of line. A print, usually of flowers, may often be mistaken for painting, because it was a Lowestoft practice often to reinforce the design with added blue pigment.

Polychrome decoration was confined to a very few styles, the most common of which features a Chinese root ornament, full of holes, from which project sprays of flowers, and sometimes a fence, in the characteristic enamels of opaque blue, emerald green and red. Flower-painting was done in conventional style, usually featuring roses, the blooms mere blobs of enamel, and the leaves drawn with a single brush-stroke. The central motif of carelessly painted bouquets is usually a pair of roses, placed back to back, and Chinese figure painting is of Chinese mandarins drawn large, in reserves enclosed by black diaper and scroll borders. The Lowestoft borders, in fact, are very similar to those used at New Hall, and were it not for the difference between the soft and hard pastes the two porcelains might very easily be confused with each other. Most commonly seen is a band of elementary pink scale, and others include a dotted wavy line intersecting a wavy line of flower-sprays, and a carmine looped ribbon interrupted by flowers.

CHAPTER TEN

Plymouth, Bristol and New Hall porcelain

TRUE or hard-paste porcelain was made in this country at Plymouth, Bristol and New Hall in Staffordshire, in that order, and the man who at last discovered Böttger's sixty-year-old secret was William Cookworthy, a chemist of Plymouth. It was in 1768, after nearly twenty years of experiment, that he first used china-clay and china-stone to make porcelain. In 1770 he moved his factory to Bristol, and three years later sold out to Richard Champion, his partner.

We have already seen how in Liverpool and elsewhere the greatest threat to the porcelain makers' livelihood was Wedgwood's cream-ware, and it was Wedgwood who in 1775 led a movement to cut off Champion's supplies of raw materials. There was legal action, and Champion won, but it was so obvious to him that he could not compete with the Potteries that in 1781 he in turn sold out to a syndicate of potters who continued to make hard-paste at New Hall.

To the expert there are many points of difference between the wares made at the three different factories and at different periods, but it will be sufficient for our purpose to divide them into three classes—Cookworthy's, Champion's, and New Hall. Identification of all three depends above all on the ability to recognize a true porcelain, and only experience can teach it. Nevertheless, the points to look for, the hardness, the cold appearance, the characteristic appearance of the enamels, and so on will be discussed at greater length in a later chapter. When once they are fully understood it is a question of handling as many pieces as possible.

There is really little danger of mistaking English true porcelain for that which was made in the Far East or on the Continent.

The most enthusiastic admirer of Plymouth or Bristol ware will admit that there is really no comparison. After all, Cookworthy was an experimenter, his successors never fully mastered the correct proportions of china-clay and china-stone, and the result was that the wares were always prone to warping and cracking in the kiln, with truly round, level plates or dishes the exception, and with a tendency towards black spotting, yellow staining, and foot-rims speckled with sand. The spiral ridges or 'wreathing' inside turned vessels, left by the potter's fingers, is not a defect, but it is certainly a valuable aid to identification.

These imperfections apart, the Plymouth and Bristol paste is dead white, at best very like Bristol opaque white glass. Its glaze is thin and quite colourless, though it is sometimes milky in the crevices, due to the presence of tiny air-bubbles. The translucency is clear, with a faint tinge of the palest grey.

Much of Cookworthy's first porcelain was painted in under-glaze blue, and the designs were copied from Lowestoft, Worcester and Bow wares in a pigment that is usually greyish-blue in tone, sometimes nearly black. The polychrome decoration, on the other hand, is outstanding in design; it is rare to find a piece upon which the decoration hides too much of the porcelain, There is always balance. The flower-painting is simple, usually composed of crescent-shaped sprays accompanied by sprigs and insects, in opaque blues and greens, and a good yellow. The exotic bird is often seen, and the naturalistic one (somewhat stylized and having a 'stuffed' appearance), and many designs were copied from the oriental, including figures in land-scapes, and such famille-verte patterns as the 'kylin', more common on Worcester porcelain. The early gilding has often disappeared, or at least is badly rubbed, and the gold rims preferred by other factories are replaced by brown or red edged ones. For the most part the shapes of domestic wares differ little from those used elsewhere, but mention must be made of Cookworthy's large hexagonal vases, garnitures of vases and beakers, and centre-pieces modelled in the form of scallop-shells, tiered, and studded with smaller shells of all kinds.

The figures of the period suffer from warping and fire-cracking, but they are well-modelled and less idyllic as regards costume than their gay Chelsea and Derby counterparts. Their bases are either scrolled in the rococo style or rectangular, and a characteristic feature is that the applied flowers are trumpet-shaped. Mention has been made elsewhere of the sets of 'Continents' which so resemble those made at Longton Hall.

Figure 17. A Plymouth 'salt'.

Champion's proprietorship brought about a gradual improvement, both technically and aesthetically. Inevitably, much less blue-painting was done, though a little blue-printing was attempted until it was proved that the hard paste did not take kindly to the process. We now see for the first time the typical Bristol enamelled festoons of flowers, mostly in green, and greatly improved exotic birds, quite equal to those done at Worcester, because the same artists painted some of them, either in decorating studios or in the factories during the course of their wanderings. Ground colours were brought into use, in yellow, brown, pink, ruby and crimson, and the gilding, often applied over red enamel to give it depth, is second to none.

The same improvement is seen in Champion's figures, which are never gaudy, and are never backed by the bocage which was so popular at Chelsea and Derby. The bases are simple, with no rococo scrolls, and unlike the earlier ones they are closed. Bristol rarities which will probably not come the way of the beginner, but which are important enough to command attention, are the wonderfully modelled white biscuit plaques, featur-

Figure 18. New Hall tea-pot in Chinese style.

ing heraldic shields, portraits, initials and flowers, each petal of which was separately and most delicately modelled after nature. In order properly to appreciate their beauty it is really necessary to use a magnifying glass.

After the move to New Hall, figures were not made by the new proprietors, who concentrated upon domestic wares of markedly inferior quality, made of a dirty grey paste which usually gives a pale yellow translucency. Despite their early origin and nature, New Hall wares can never be mistaken for Plymouth or Bristol, for apart from the inferior paste and skimped glaze, ground colours and the finer styles of decoration were entirely given up. Instead, a new range of simple designs was evolved, based it would seem on Lowestoft and 'export Chinese' models, sketchily painted and possessing little artistic merit. Floral designs are predominant, with usually a pair of back-to-back roses, and scattered sprigs, with no attempt at botanical accuracy. Another favourite pattern has as its central motif a basket of flowers, and mandarin designs are common, painted in the usual factory palette of a peculiar dark puce, a dirty blue, brick-red, green and yellow, though the 'basket' pattern in particular was sometimes painted in black and gold. Borders are similar to those used at Lowestoft, but others include blue trellis or circles between red lines, and two intersecting wavy lines.

Shapes are typical, and usually lead to easy identification, even without the help of the patterns. Tea-pots were made straight-sided and lobed, in silver style, elliptic and ogee-shaped, elliptic with vertical sides, and boat-shaped with raised rims thrusting upwards at the spout ends, and rising smoothly to merge into the handles. Cream jugs were made to match, and helmet-shaped ones, similar to those made at Liverpool, are fairly common.

It is well to remember that hard-paste was discarded at New Hall in 1810, but that the same shapes and styles of decoration were continued for another fifteen years, an ordinary bone-ash paste being used.

CHAPTER ELEVEN

Nantgarw and Swansea porcelain

THERE were some early nineteenth-century potters who were not content to adopt the new bone-ash body which had been adopted throughout the industry. They compared it with the wonderful soft-paste of Sèvres, and they could not resist the urge to try to make something as good, if only because they knew that the London dealers would pay well for it.

One such man was William Billingsley, whose working life was spent in wandering from one place to another, sometimes as master (as at Pinxton where he first succeeded in making a porcelain fine enough to satisfy him) and sometimes as man. His genius and his unquenchable enthusiasm made its mark at Derby, Worcester and Coalport, that we know, and if legend be believed he worked at other places also. That he never became rich, and that he was unable to keep his head above water for very long, was because he was trying to make an impossibly expensive porcelain at a time when other manufacturers were content to make a serviceable, adequately decorated ware in large quantities.

Billingsley left his employment at Worcester in November 1813, taking Samuel Walker, his son-in-law with him, to set up a factory in Nantgarw, near Cardiff. A year passed, and having asked in vain for government financial aid he was helped by their investigator, a potter named Dillwyn, owner of the Swansea 'Cambrian Pottery', who invited the two men to make their porcelain there. All went well until the end of 1816, when an unexpected difficulty arose. Apparently when Billingsley left Worcester he had come to an agreement with his old employers which gave them the right to complain about his association with Dillwyn. The result was that poor Billingsley was forced to return to Nantgarw, where he struggled on until 1819. Thus we have the three periods of his Welsh venture: Nantgarw

1813–14, Swansea 1814–16, Nantgarw 1816–19. It is surely food for thought to contrast that kind of pillar to post existence, filled as it must have been with constant anxiety in an attempt to make ends meet, with the remarkable ware that was made under such conditions.

The basis of the Billingsley porcelain made at both places

Figure 19. Nantgarw handled goblet.

was the experimental paste first evolved at Pinxton, and improved during the first Nantgarw period. It was of the bone-ash variety, containing china-clay and a glassy fritt. No paste, not even the finest soft-paste Sèvres, has a purer, clearer, white translucency, with no cloudiness, no granularity and, at best, no sanding, staining, or pitting. This was clearly achieved, however, only at the expense of ruinous kiln losses, and we do very occasionally come across a piece which had to be decorated, even though it was fire-cracked. Billingsley's glaze is absolutely clear and colourless, glistening, and pleasantly smooth and satisfying to the touch. Of these two component parts the Nantgarw wares were made, seventy-five per cent of which were plates and dishes, the rest being small decorative pieces such as spill-vases, tazzas, candlesticks, tankards, pen-trays, and tea and dessert services. Most of the Billingsley forms naturally resemble those made at Sèvres, with moulded, scrolled rims, pie-crust edges, or wide rims left perfectly plain. When there is moulding it is usually so pronounced that it can be felt and seen on the underside.

Some Nantgarw porcelain was factory decorated, a very few pieces by Billingsley himself, but much more was decorated in London in those French styles which the dealers knew would command a ready sale, with much use of ground colours and gold. A great deal of ware which was left behind when Billingsley left the district to go to Coalport was decorated by Thomas Pardoe, between about 1820 and 1822.

A peculiarity of much Nantgarw porcelain is the presence of iridescence which may extend over the whole piece, affect only small areas, or surround the enamelling like a halo. It has now been decided that this feature signifies that the decoration was done in London, and that it is never found on the factory decorated wares that are more desirable to the collector. Indeed, the Nantgarw lover has to contend with the fact that the characteristic mouldings were used not only at Coalport (whither Billingsley took his moulds and his engraved copper plates of marks), but elsewhere, and for that reason the impressed mark NANTGARW, with or without the letters CW, has considerable value to him. It is a mark which can very easily be overlooked, because it is often entirely filled with glaze.

It was probably on Dillwyn's insistence that Billingsley took steps at Swansea to make his paste less expensive to produce, and the first result, about 1816, was the 'duck-egg' porcelain, so called because of its unmistakable, rather cloudy, greenish translucency. A year later came the still cheaper but inferior 'trident' body (marked with one or two impressed tridents)

PLATE I

Left: Lowestoft jug with mask-lip and moulded body painted in underglaze blue in the Chinese style. About 1765. *Below:* Ralph Wood toby jugs; 'The Squire' and 'Earl Howe' decorated with coloured glazes. About 1760–70.

PLATE II

Left: Wedgwood black basalte lamp in the classical style. About 1783. (Nottingham Museum.) *Right*: Derby vase;

PLATE III

Left: Toft ware; decorated with brown slip on a yellow-brown body in typical style. About 1660–80. *Right*: Blue dash charger, probably Bristol, decorated with an 'Adam and Eve' subject. About 1640–50.

PLATE IV

Right: Spode plate; printed in under-glaze blue with a scene representing the Landing of the Pilgrim Fathers. About 1830.

Left: Bristol plate; painted with flowers and ribbon border. About 1770–80. (Winifred Williams.)

PLATE VI

Left: Leeds creamware cruet; a typical example of pierced decoration. About 1780. *Below:* Worcester fruit dish; painted with 'exotic birds' in a panel reserved on an apple-green ground. About 1770. (Victoria and Albert Museum.)

PLATE VIII

Above: Longton Hall porcelain; painted in various styles. About 1753–5. (Victoria and Albert Museum.) *Below:* Pratt trinket set; printed with scenes of ruins reserved on a turquoise ground. About 1855.

which apparently pleased Dillwyn, but certainly not the dealers, who naturally disliked its yellowish translucency and its rather matt, pitted glaze. They were interested only in something which would compete with the French wares, and without their approval and support Billingsley's venture was doomed to failure.

The styles favoured by the Swansea management (for we have to remember that Billingsley was not his own master) were

Figure 20. Swansea tureen and cover.

similar to those which had proved to be acceptable on the Nant-garw ware, but with certain changes and additions. Large jugs were made (which are difficult to separate from those made at Coalport) and moulded plates and dishes, though the emphasis was transferred from them to dessert- and tea-sets. Much extremely fine flower-painting was done, and it must be supposed that Billingsley, relieved somewhat from the cares of responsible management, was able to devote more time to the training of his painters. But still, even at Swansea, he himself rarely painted, and the fine decoration we now admire was done by, amongst others, William Pollard (flowers and fruit), David Evans (flowers and fruit), George Beddow (landscapes), Henry Morris (bouquets) and Thomas Baxter (landscapes and gardens).

It should be stressed once again that because Billingsley went to Coalport much of the porcelain made there is of such fine quality that it passes very well as Swansea or even, occasionally, as Nantgarw. Thus the collector has to guard against wishful thinking, and to try to collect, and indeed to study while he is learning, only those pieces which bear the impressed marks, which of course could not easily be imitated.

CHAPTER TWELVE

Other porcelains

IT is convenient here to discuss the Pinxton porcelain mentioned in the previous chapter, made at a short-lived factory set up in 1796 by John Coke, for the purpose of working Billingsley's formula. Billingsley left Pinxton not later than 1801, after which inferior ware of no importance was made, until the factory closed about 1813.

We naturally expect to find a close resemblance between the Pinxton porcelain and that made in Wales; it is perfectly white, has a slightly greenish or pinkish translucency, and was very liable to warping in the kiln. The decoration follows much on Derby lines, and indeed a number of workmen accompanied Billingsley to his new works, including the famous modeller, W. Coffee, and the landscape painters Edward Rowland and James Hadfield. Another landscape painter, John Cutts, later became proprietor of the factory, and he is best known for his painting on the scarce Wedgwood porcelain. At Pinxton he specialized in local views, rather sketchily drawn, and favouring pale reds and yellowish greens. Much of the decoration, and the landscapes in particular, are often reserved in gold foliate frames upon coloured grounds of poor quality in pinkish fawn, yellow and green. Sprigged patterns such as the underglaze blue 'Tournay sprig' and the 'Paris cornflower' in blue, green and pink, bordered with blue or brown lines, were much used upon domestic wares.

Among the many factories about which little is known apart from unreliable legend are those at which Billingsley is reputed to have made porcelain. We know that he left Pinxton to go to Mansfield, but only to paint upon ware brought in the white from the Potteries. Thence he moved to Torksey, in Lincolnshire, and at some time or other he is said to have worked at Wirksworth in Derbyshire, with the result that from time to time, on very little real evidence, pieces turn up which are claimed to have been made at one or other of these places. Tradition has similarly attributed a few kinds of porcelain with Church Gresley, near Burton-on-Trent, including parts of a dessert-service painted with yellow panels alternating with panels of flowers—the 'Church Gresley pattern'. It would appear that porcelain was probably made there—from 1794 to 1808—but these pieces are almost certainly of Worcester (Flights) or even Derby origin, and the true ware still remains to be finally identified.

We are on very different ground when we turn to another porcelain that was made as the result of rebellion against the general early nineteenth-century trend. It was made at Rockingham between about 1820 and 1842, under the patronage of the Earl Fitzwilliam. Here the inspiration was not supplied by a genius who aimed high regardless of fame or success, but by a nobleman who was willing to pay for the prestige that was accorded to him as the result of his fashionable hobby. The result was the same, a porcelain finer than its contemporaries, at any rate as regards decoration, very expensive to produce, and destined at length, if not to ruin, at least to discourage its makers. Thus, John and William Brameld began the work in the Swinton premises where cream-ware had been made since 1778. William's sons followed on, and in 1830 a Royal Warrant was granted, probably on account of a service costing £5,000 which was made for William IV, and which was so extravagantly painted that it virtually closed the factory.

Throughout, once production of a good paste had been achieved, extravagance was the keynote—over-elaborate modelling, ostentatious decoration, splendid ground colours, and profuse coppery gilding—not only on services intended for the Earl's immediate circle of friends, but also on domestic wares intended for general sale.

The Rockingham paste is with difficulty distinguishable from those of Coalport, Davenport and other top-flight contemporary factories; a bone-ash composition, very white, covered with a thin and lustrous glaze (which sometimes crazed), and having a pale yellow translucency. The decoration, on the other hand, has many distinguishing features, apart from its lavishness. Tea services were made in large numbers, since the ceremony of the afternoon tea-table was of great importance in Society. Some are painted with careful little landscape vignettes, upon ground colours of dark, opaque apple-green, Reckitt's blue, neutral grey, magenta or pale yellow, and others with scrolls or flower-sprays either in gold or in pale yellow edged with gold, upon a broad band of ground colour. This pale yellow, with gold, is in fact commonly seen as a foil to a stronger colour, magenta

Figure 21. Rockingham cottage.

in particular. Flowers and landscapes comprise most of the Rockingham decoration upon all kinds of services and upon many large vases, and applied flowers in the Coalport style are often found in conjunction with either or both.

No figures of any consequence were made, but in fact many crudely modelled late Staffordshire ones have been mistakenly classified as Rockingham, simply because of the presence upon their bases, or upon their costume, of a particularly dark mazarine blue which is occasionally found upon true Rockingham wares. Nevertheless, we may credit to the factory some pastille-burners or 'cottages' which are always carefully modelled, some of them in a very fine and much coveted lavender-coloured paste, with applied flowers and 'moss', and a wide range of sheep and dogs, the paste pricked out to resemble wool or curly hair, and glazed all over. The famous streaky brown Rockingham glaze, perfected for use on the earlier earthenware, was used on the porcelain, beautifully graduated from dark to light on the outsides of the articles, and relieved by thin gold lines at the rims.

Though Wedgwood is a name to conjure with in all ceramic circles, the management was always so preoccupied with the making of cream-ware and jasper that porcelain was neglected until about 1810. The ware then made, but only for a short time, was a true porcelain, well-decorated in the contemporary style, mostly with flowers and landscapes, and of no outstanding merit. The collector must take care not to confuse it with the Wedgwood semi-translucent stoneware.

Josiah Spode the Second began to make porcelain at Stoke-on-Trent just before the end of the eighteenth century. It was he, of course, who was responsible for perfecting the bone-ash paste which became the standard one throughout the Potteries, and about 1825 the addition of felspar to the formula resulted in an even more durable ware. The third Spode porcelain was given the name of 'bone china', but it was really a hybrid, part earthenware and part porcelain, which was used for the cheaper but still well-decorated wares.

The Spode decorators adopted any and every style, whatever its origin, which proved to be popular at any given time. They took the Bloor Derby 'Japans' and some of the early Worcester ones, and improved upon them, and they used good ground colours of pale green, grey, biscuit, fawn, and bright yellow in conjunction with panels of flower painting in the style of Sèvres and Coalport. Blue-printing was developed to the extreme, with a multiplicity of patterns, mostly in the Nankin style, and overglaze enamel printing was used to outline designs which were then filled in with enamels. This process was nothing new in the industry, but it was used by Spodes to afford a large number of different colour schemes from a single print. The patterns first used were Chinese, but the same system was used later, especially on the 'bone china', for every other style of decoration. A fine body called 'Parian' was introduced in 1846, marble-like and very suitable for figures, in imitation of the famous Derby biscuit.

Thomas Minton, the pupil of Turner at Caughley, opened his Stoke factory in 1796, and it has flourished ever since. His

Figure 22. A Spode 'Japan' pattern.

porcelain was of the usual bone-ash variety, apart from an experimental hard-paste which was made round about 1850. Decoration is invariably of the highest quality, but there is little about it which serves to distinguish the porcelain from that made in other comparable factories, with the possible exception of an outstanding turquoise enamel often found as a border on domestic ware, or as an effective relief to the white austerity of a Parian body which was as good as that made by Spodes. A fine 'stone china' was usually decorated in Chinese styles, among which the 'Amherst Japan' is best known. We must also mention the Minton *pâte sur pâte* style of decoration, introduced at the factory by M. L. Solon of Sèvres, in which successive layers of white clay upon, usually, a pale sage-green ground produce an effect very similar to that achieved by Bott at Worcester, on his 'Limoges enamels'.

Davenport porcelain has quite recently come very much to the fore among nineteenth-century wares. The factory was founded in 1793, at Longport, by John Davenport, and work was carried on until 1887. During such a long life it is obvious that a very considerable amount of porcelain must have been made, but because so much is unmarked it has been credited to other factories, usually Worcester or Coalport. Indeed, there is really no sure way of identifying it, though it may be said that there is a general tendency towards the use of a very strong underglaze blue, with deep red and a great deal of gilding upon Japan patterns, and a marked preference for making large dessert services. Upon these we find excellent grounds of Reckitt's blue, Rose du Barry and celadon green, upon which naturalistic flower-painting (some probably by Thomas Steele of Derby) and landscapes by Mountford are reserved.

One of the many factories which flourished during the latter half of the nineteenth century, where fine porcelain was made but about which very little is known by the average collector, was the Hanley factory of Cauldon Place, originally founded by Job Ridgway in 1802. The body of this (usually marked) ware is of the ordinary bone-ash type, but the decoration applied to it is invariably of outstanding excellence. The ground colours are unusually even and pure, the gilding either matt or burnished, and applied very thickly. A feature of many dessert services, which were made in great quantities, is the imaginative treatment of the rims of plates, dishes and comports. One design has an outer rim which is formed of loops of 'ribbon' standing out from the normal edge, for instance, while another rim is outlined with projecting rays of the 'jewels' or beads of porcelain which were used commonly as a foil to coloured grounds. The high quality of the factory's productions may be judged from the fact that in 1877 a splendid dessert service was made for the Prince of Wales, painted with different hunting scenes.

So we come to the end of our discussion of English and Welsh porcelains, but it must be remembered that it is on record that in 1852 there were upwards of 130 potteries in Staffordshire, apart from those in other parts of Britain. The inference is that there is an ever-present danger of attributing a piece of porcelain to one or other of the leading factories, about which we know a great deal, whereas in fact there were undoubtedly many smaller concerns who were quite capable of making wares of equal merit. Some day, perhaps, they may be given the credit due to them, but that time is not yet. In the meantime, correct attribution (or indeed attribution that may often be influenced by wishful thinking) is doubtless a satisfying thing, but the collector ought not to stress its importance so highly that he loses sight of what, after all, is the greatest joy of his hobby—the possession and the enjoyment of beautiful things.

CHAPTER THIRTEEN

Lead-glazed earthenwares

IT is not always easy to decide whether the decoration upon a piece of porcelain or earthenware is of greater importance than the piece itself, than some peculiar nature of the ware or, it may be, some point of rarity that transcends mere beauty. A great deal depends on individual interests, for whereas one collector may be fascinated with factory history, the nature of pastes and glazes, or the derivation of shapes and forms, another may be of such an aesthetic turn of mind that the decoration is everything, and the ware itself merely the canvas upon which it was painted or applied. Sometimes the two are happily married, and the ornamentation has the effect of drawing attention, not only to the beautiful surface of the ware but also to every subtle curve of its shape. The Chinese knew the secret, and so, too, did some of the early delft and porcelain makers, even when they were not making exact copies of oriental models, but as time went on and technical difficulties were overcome, it all became almost too easy, and the art of the potter became subservient to that of the decorator.

It is true to say, I think, that part of the charm of the medieval lead-glazed earthenware is due to the fact that it was not at all easy to decorate it. Indeed, there were no decorators as we understand the term. The potter made his ware of whatever kind of clay came to hand, his fingers pressed, and ridged, and pinched to impart some kind of ornament, helped perhaps by a bit of stick, a sharp flint, or a pretty sea-shell, and he then covered the whole with a thick, glassy glaze which effectively discouraged any kind of brushwork. His only mechanical aid was the potter's wheel.

It would be wrong to expect that medieval wares are necessarily monotonously lacking in colour, however. The potter could use clays of different colours, red, black, grey, buff and so on, and he could stain his glaze yellow or green. His applied blobs, bars and rings could be made of a colour different from that of the body. If he scratched (or 'incised') designs in his ware they could be filled in, again, with a different kind of clay, and above all he made great use of 'slip', a liquid form of clay which he could pour out in any kind of design, in just the same way as a confectioner ices a cake. This slip-ware, as it is called, attracts because of the clever use of contrasting but always mellow colours.

The story really begins when nomadic potters, about six hundred years ago, settled for a while in places where their services were needed—at the monasteries. We see some of their work on the floors of such buildings as Great Malvern Priory and Chertsey Abbey, the wonderful tiles decorated in every kind of heraldic, legendary, or floral and foliate style. The potter cut or pressed his designs into his flat slabs of brown clay, filled them in with white clay, ground them smooth, and glazed them. We call them 'encaustic' or 'burnt in' tiles.

Whenever such a potter moved to a new place where there was suitable clay he made ware for the countryfolk or townsfolk which, apparently, mostly took the form of tall jugs or pitchers. At any rate, so we may judge from the quantity that has been excavated; for, of course, long-disused wells and rubbish-heaps are the kinds of places whence existing specimens have come. The earliest thirteenth-century examples are tall and slender, well-nigh cylindrical but swelling out slightly at the waist, and very plain. We can still see how the potter's fingers ridged the body or pinched out a lip, and how his spatulate thumb pulled down the clay of the handle to make a firm joint. Gradually, during the fourteenth century, the bodies of the jugs became more swollen, and the resultant greater stability was sometimes further increased when the potter thumbed down his clay around his base, incidentally adding decoration to his ware. In addition, he added impressed and incised designs of circles, triangles, diamonds, and bands of trellis-work, and applied pads of clay roughly fashioned into the forms of animals, birds, flower-sprays, and rosettes. His coloured glazes were sometimes manipulated to cover only a portion of the ware.

Improvement during the fifteenth and sixteenth centuries followed on natural lines, and by the beginning of the seventeenth a large range of articles was being made in slip-ware, including plates, dishes, jugs, cups, posset-pots and loving-cups. No other country has ever produced anything quite like it, and it certainly owed nothing to any foreign source. Its attraction lies in its subdued colours, for few of the shapes could be called beautiful. Its making was indeed a purely country craft, for the few potteries which had been established supplied only their immediate surroundings. There was as yet no ceramic industry. Comparatively few examples of this early date now exist, for slip-ware was utilitarian and expendable, but there are some which, by the presence upon them of names, initials or dates, seem to have been made for some special occasion, such as a birth, a christening or a marriage.

Best known of this rare kind of ware are those pieces which have been given the name of 'Toft Ware', because the names of Ralph or Thomas Toft are sometimes found upon them. It has never been certainly decided whether in fact there were any potters so named working at that time, and the question remains, did they make them, or were they the recipients? Whichever way it may be, these clumsily potted pieces, mostly large 'platters' (round dishes), are all decorated in the same way, with a profusion of trellis-work, and featuring flowers and leaves, mermaids, heraldic lions, royalty, the 'Pelican in her Piety', and Adam and Eve, either in white slip on red, or vice versa. Another contemporary slip-ware, called 'Metropolitan Ware' because it has been unearthed in London, betrays the Puritan influence by the religious flavour of its inscriptions, and a third, 'Wrotham Ware', apparently made near Wrotham in Kent, is decorated in a style which would have appealed to rustic users—the inscriptions are bucolic and the decorative motifs after nature, mostly in floral or foliate style.

Later seventeenth- and eighteenth-century slip-wares are

much more simple and restrained from the decorative point of view, with a great deal of free drawing of flower-sprays, simple scrolls, and symmetrical posy arrangements, usually in white slip on a red ground. A new process was introduced, in which several layers of liquid slip of different colours were mingled together while still fluid, by means of wooden combs. Wares so treated are called 'combed' or 'feathered', and it must be empha-

Figure 23. Fremington puzzle-jug.

sized that they were made well into the nineteenth century, as indeed were other kinds of slip-ware, at such places as Barnstaple, Ticknall in Derbyshire, and Black Burton in Yorkshire. Some of these late pieces have misleading (earlier) dates.

Another eighteenth-century slip-ware was made in imitation of an Italian ware, and so it has been given the Italian name of 'sgraffito', which means 'scratched'. The process by which it was made was similar to that used for making combed wares, with the difference that the clay was allowed to dry before a design was cut through tle top layer, to reveal another colour beneath. The designs vary ittle from those found upon other kinds of slip-ware, and it was made in Devonshire, at Barnstaple, Bideford and Fremington.

Whereas all the slip-wares we have considered were the products of local rural craftsmen, we now turn to those made in the Potteries, under something approaching factory conditions.

Figure 24. Whieldon 'cauliflower' ware.

The name most intimately connected with them is that of Thomas Whieldon (1719–95) who was for some time senior partner to the great Josiah Wedgwood. Above all, Whieldon was initially responsible for the development of coloured, transparent lead glazes. He stained them blue-grey, purple-brown, yellow-brown, and green with metallic oxides, and their beauty has never been equalled on any kind of pottery, though as might be expected they were closely rivalled by Wedgwood, the green in particular.

This was a copper-oxide pigment, seen at its best on Whieldon articles in the shapes of maize-cobs, cauliflowers and pineapples, the upper portions of pale yellow. Whieldon 'tortoise-shell' wares are equally well known, and their mottled coloured-glaze appearance was obtained by adding a colourless glaze to oxides of cobalt (blue), copper (green), and manganese (purple-brown) which were applied to the ware in powder form. A different kind of blending, this time of clays of different colours, was used to produce the 'solid agate' wares which were an improvement on rather similar work done by the earlier slip-ware makers.

A potter whose work is closely associated with Whieldon's was John Astbury (1688–1743), so much so that in many cases a ware may be classified under the name of Astbury-Whieldon. It was Astbury who was responsible for the process of 'sprigging' which was used extensively by Whieldon, a process by which small stamped reliefs of vine leaves and grapes, flowers and leaves, and animal forms were applied to the body of the ware. Ware so treated is found in many varieties, all relying upon contrast of colour for their effect, using clays ranging from very pale buff to orange, brown, green and red. Occasionally a black body was used, very like that of Jackfield, and there was sometimes a sparing use of sized (unfired) gilding.

Astbury-Whieldon cream jugs and coffee-pots made in the sprigged style are usually of contemporary silver shape, loop-handled, with pear-shaped bodies supported on three mask-and-claw feet. Tea-pots are usually globular, with 'crabstock' handles and spouts, modelled in the gnarled shape of a branch of a crab-apple tree. These handles are usually of the same colour as the sprigged ornament. It is noteworthy that most of these lead-glazed pieces have their counterparts among contemporary salt-glazed pieces. That is because the same body (and the same potting and decorative techniques) were used for both, in the same factories, the only difference being the kind of glaze that was used.

CHAPTER FOURTEEN

Salt-glazed stonewares

IF a hard earthenware is fired at a very high temperature it becomes semi-vitreous, non-porous and, sometimes, semi-translucent. There is no practical need to glaze it, but it was discovered in the fifteenth century, in Germany, that if common salt were introduced into the kiln at a certain temperature the result was a dully lustrous, slightly pitted surface, almost like orange-skin, that was extremely decorative. Wine made in Germany was in fact exported in Elizabethan times in bottles made of salt-glazed stoneware, and a London potter named John Dwight obtained patents from Charles II for making a stoneware that is difficult to distinguish from the foreign. Best known of the latter wares are the grotesque 'Bellarmines' or 'Greybeards' which bear a caricature mask of an unpopular cardinal of the time, but many English examples, probably made in Fulham, are quite plain, made of a brown or fawn-coloured clay, while rarer examples bear applied or modelled Tudor roses, coats-of-arms or portrait medallions.

To revert to John Dwight, the speciality which resulted from his 1671 patent was a greyish-white or pale buff stoneware, thinly salt-glazed from which he made not only domestic wares but also figures which will be described in a later chapter. He made also a certain amount of ware of red clay, decorated with stamped ornament, though in this regard he is not so well known as the famous Elers brothers, John and David, who were making stoneware some twenty years after Dwight began. Specimens usually credited to them include tea-pots, coffee-pots and cream jugs, some of them of silver shape, which imitated (and are difficult to distinguish from) those made by the Chinese and, later, by Böttger of Meissen. They are unglazed, engine-turned or decorated with stamped applied ornament in Chinese style, or with flowers and scrollwork, and are sometimes marked with pseudo-Chinese seals. The Elers made stoneware in black also, very like the later black basalt made at Etruria by Wedgwood. John Astbury, who legend says was for some time assistant to the Elers brothers, not only made similar wares, but also others of different coloured clays—fawn, brown and orange, which

Figure 25. White salt-glaze candlestick.

were decorated in exactly the same style as his lead-glazed wares. Early stoneware was not made only at Fulham. It would seem that in Staffordshire a variety of it, known as 'Crouch Ware', was made before 1690, and other centres were at Lambeth, Bampton, Mortlake and Nottingham, where many of the grotesque 'Bear Jugs' were produced.

The lovely white salt-glazed ware of Staffordshire was made from about 1720 onwards, after some potter, probably Astbury, following upon Dwight's methods, mixed ordinary clay with sand or calcined flint and white pipe-clay. The result was a fine white body which, as we have already seen, could be salt-glazed or lead-glazed and which was a much better substitute for Chinese porcelain than those which had gone before. Thin potting and lightness of weight are both characteristic of the early Staffordshire salt-glaze, which was made in moulds of metal or alabaster which imparted a fine sharpness of detail. As time went on these were replaced by cheaper plaster moulds, with the result that this early characteristic was lost. Some of the more unusual pieces, such as tea-pots shaped like warships, camels, houses, squirrels, and so on, or sensible domestic wares such as mugs, tea-caddies, basins, sauce-boats and tureens were made by the casting process. In this case, instead of clay being pressed against a one-piece mould, it was poured in slip form into a two-piece one, which absorbed the water until the desired thickness of body was obtained. The surplus slip was then poured off, and the two halves of the mould separated. A great deal of ware was sprigged with applied ornaments, as distinct from the earlier process in which reliefs were stamped directly on the body, in the forms of vine, scrolls and lacework, and Chinese prunus blossom. Crabstock tea-pots and other domestic wares resemble in shape those which were lead-glazed, for reasons already discussed. An early attempt at colour, between 1745 and 1750, at a time when quality was deteriorating, and when the rather monotonous decorative forms of basketwork, rococo scrolling and trelliswork were fashionable, was the use of the sgraffito technique described in the previous chapter, but in this case the incised designs were filled in with cobalt blue. Mention should be made also of the first use by William Littler of the strong 'Littler's Blue' used later on his porcelain, either applied in moulded panels or else covering an entire surface.

The true splendour of Staffordshire salt-glazed stoneware is to be enjoyed on wares made from about 1750 onwards. It is recorded that about that time two Dutchmen built enamelling kilns at Cobridge for the purpose of decorating salt-glazed wares, for it was found that their surface imparted to the enamels a much greater brilliance than could be obtained on any other kind of body. The result is that painting upon white salt-glaze has a jewel-like appearance, with no sinking into the glaze, that is unequalled even on the finest porcelain. The styles of decoration favoured by these pioneers, and by others who quickly came into the Potteries from Bristol, Liverpool and London (where the

Figure 26. Coloured salt-glaze.

delft painters had congregated) naturally resembles those found on contemporary English porcelain. We find countless adaptations of oriental themes, landscapes, bold flower-painting, pastoral subjects after Watteau and Boucher in the Sèvres style, and portraits of Royalty. Finest of all are those rare pieces on which panels of enamelled decoration are reserved upon strong ground colours of green, crimson, pink, blue or turquoise.

Staffordshire salt-glazed stoneware fell from popular favour with the perfecting of Wedgwood's cream-ware and the porcelain made at Worcester and Derby. The body, or rather a debased, crude form of it, was used for many years to make only drain-pipes and ginger-beer bottles. In the mid-nineteenth century, however, Henry Doulton of Lambeth began to make ornamental vases and plaques in a heavy brown stoneware, decorated with incised patterns, and painted in brown, blue, fawn and green. Some of these were exhibited in 1871 at the South Kensington Exhibition, and Queen Victoria described them as being 'honest, useful and in thoroughly good taste'. We should perhaps disagree with such a sweeping statement, at least as far as good taste is concerned, for much of the ware is over-decorated, but several of Doulton's designers, the Barlows and George Tinworth in particular, did in fact produce a great deal of restrained, well-drawn decoration. However that may be, there was a revival of interest in stoneware as a result of the Royal approval, and among those who took advantage of it was Robert Martin, a sculptor, who with his brothers Edwin, Walter and Charles set up a pottery in 1873 which flourished for over forty years. Their brown, salt-glazed wares, all of them marked, are characterized above all by their elaborate modelling, though many pieces have incised decoration in the Doulton style. Best known of their wares are the jugs and vases modelled in the shapes of beasts, birds, monsters or even public notabilities, some with detachable heads, caricatured, with their faces bearing every kind of grotesque expression.

English delftware

THE tin-glazed earthenware which is called delft in Holland and in this country, majolica in Italy, and faience in Germany and France was the early eighteenth-century potter's answer to the popular demand for decorative Chinese porcelain, or for something which looked like it. Western eyes had been opened, as early as the fifteenth century, to the fact that pottery could be ornamental as well as useful, but only the very rich could afford the thin, translucent, beautifully enamelled oriental porcelain that found its way by devious and expensive routes into Europe. There had to be a substitute of some kind, but though the covering of ordinary earthenware by a lead glaze containing tin oxide did produce a white surface, it was a substitute that was still necessarily clumsily potted and that was not translucent. It was therefore inevitable that with the successful making of porcelain in this country, and of its rival, cream-ware, delft making came to an end.

From the technical point of view, delft was made of a soft-clay body, fired at a low temperature, and covered with the tin glaze, which was then left to dry. The painted decoration was then applied, to a surface which was very absorbent, even powdery and loose, and which could be worked upon only with bold, sweeping strokes of the brush. It was like painting on blotting-paper, and intricate detail could never be attempted. The glaze had to be fired at a high temperature, and in those days the only colours which would survive the heat were iron-reds, antimony yellows, cobalt blues, manganese browns and purpies, and copper green. Such a palette provided the delft painter with opportunity to produce colourful but not subtle designs.

The delft-making industry in this country seems to have begun when two potters from Antwerp, Jaspar Andries and Jacob Janson, petitioned Queen Elizabeth I, in 1567, to be allowed to stay in England to make what was then known as 'gallyware', but the earliest identifiable English ware, consisting of certain globular jugs, mottled in various colours, and called 'Malling Jugs', are too rare to have anything but an academic interest for the ordinary collector.

Seventeenth- and eighteenth-century delft was made at three centres, Lambeth, Bristol and Liverpool, and all were offshoots

Figure 27. Lambeth delft.

of a Southwark pottery which was founded before 1625. Roughly the dates are—Lambeth 1665, Bristol 1650, and Liverpool 1710. In addition there must have been a number of other unrecorded concerns working at the same time in the London area. At these, we suppose, were made the famous 'Blue Dash Chargers', large plates made for display purposes, decorated in blue, yellow, green and purple in various styles, but having in common the feature of rims bordered with short dashes or lines, usually in blue. Among the commoner designs are portraits of kings and queens with or without their initials, Adam and Eve, copies of religious subjects taken from engravings and 'broadsheets', arrangements of spirals, coils and whorls, and patterns of large flowers among which the tulip is most commonly found. Apart from these decorative wares the 'Lambeth' sack bottles are well known, decorated very simply in blue with the names of wines, accompanied by scrolled flourishes and, sometimes, dates. The earlier the date, the rarer and consequently the more valuable the bottle.

In general it is safe to say that English delft, wherever made, was decorated in the style of whatever Chinese porcelain was popular at any particular time. So, at Bristol, much early painting was done in blue, in very bold, almost careless style, upon a glaze which was lightly violet-blued to imitate the paste of the Chinese 'Blue Nankin'. Then followed copies of K'ang Hsi polychrome wares, usually in blue, muddy green, and dark orange-red. Within the limits of their materials the painters tried to copy faithfully from the originals, even to the flower-sprays beneath the rims of plates, although it must be remembered that many designs were copied not from actual Chinese models, but from Dutch versions of them.

Figure 28. Bristol delft.

As time passed the typical oriental land- and water-scapes were conventionalized, the pagodas translated into castle-like blocks pierced with rows of square windows, and so on, and at Liverpool and Bristol alike the seafaring activities encouraged the development of a style featuring actual ships with carefully detailed sails and rigging. Doubtless many pieces so decorated were ordered specially by sea-captains and owners.

A great deal of flower-painting was done at Bristol, most of it in the Chinese style, but much conventionalized with scattered sprays of blossoms unknown to any botanist. We find patterns of stylized buildings and trees apparently painted with a sponge, in manganese brown, which are often credited to Wincanton, in Somerset, and a range of commemorative pieces of which the best known bear representations of Lunardi's famous balloon ascent in 1784. Much use was made of simplified versions of Chinese brocaded diaper borders, and a floral and foliate border of white enamel, known as 'bianco-sopra-bianco' was pleasingly associated with good blue-painting or with Chinese landscapes in almost pastel tones of brown and yellow. Similar wares of this latter kind were made also at Liverpool and Lambeth, but the Bristol white enamel is usually more raised and so more clearly defined.

There is little technical difference between the delft made at the three main centres, though the Lambeth glaze sometimes has a faint pinkish tinge. Identification therefore depends largely on decorative styles. In general, Bristol brushwork strikes an average between a certain Liverpool strength that is sometimes almost crude, and a Lambeth attempt at neatness and attention to detail that often results in stiffness. Apart from that, geographical locality played a part, as we have already seen. Thus, a Liverpool speciality was the making of char-pots, very shallow, upright-sided vessels made in various sizes to contain the preserved fish, called char, which were caught in the Lakes. These are decorated with very crudely drawn fish. Sadler and Green had their printing works in Liverpool, and delft tiles were made in large quantities to be printed in overglaze black, green, blue, brown or red. The same enamels were used throughout the industry, but the Chinese brown border on export ware, added to prevent chipping, was copied at Liverpool in bright india-red, and at Lambeth in yellow or brown.

So much for general classification, which takes into account only the larger and best-known centres of delft-making. Among the many others we may include Glasgow (Delftfield), Brislington, Mortlock and Putney, all of which made delft of some kind, which had no particular characteristic. There are, however, certain forms and decorative styles which are commonly associated with particular factories. Large vases, some more than twelve inches in height, and often decorated with Chinese landscapes or flowers, were made at both Liverpool and Bristol, and so were puzzle-jugs, but whereas the necks of the Liverpool specimens were pierced with designs of four hearts arranged to form a circle, those of Bristol were perforated by intersecting circles. The very attractive cornucopia-shaped wall-vases, with moulded decoration of birds and flowers, hail from Liverpool, while Bristol examples are shaped like an inverted acorn, and bear simple Chinese scenes. A rare article in delft (though not so rare as the very valuable flat slabs which were used for pill-making) is the rectangular box or 'brick' with a perforated top, modelled upon a Chinese brush holder. Examples were made at all three centres, and a noteworthy point is that the Liverpool variety often has several large holes as well as the usual small ones.

CHAPTER SIXTEEN

Cream-ware

WE have seen how during the seventeenth and the first half of the eighteenth century an endless search went on for a kind of china that would meet all the requirements, technically and aesthetically, of a public who, even if they themselves did not possess fine porcelain, yet knew of its existence. In turn an answer was offered in the form of stoneware, lead-glazed earthenware and delft, but it was not until Josiah Wedgwood modified and perfected the body used by Astbury and his fellows for saltglazing that something really acceptable was evolved, something that was durable, handsome, admittedly opaque, but still capable of receiving unpretentious but pleasing decoration upon its clean, smooth, pleasingly yellowish surface.

In 1775 Champion of Bristol won his legal conflict with the Staffordshire potters, led by Wedgwood, with the result that they were forbidden to use china-clay and china-stone to make porcelain. If the decision had been reversed, true porcelain would probably have been made in the Potteries, but as it was, Wedgwood had to choose between making a fritt-paste body, which he knew was still in the experimental stage, and an improved cream-ware. He chose the latter, and he christened it 'Queen's Ware'. There is no doubt that he acted wisely, and his example was soon followed by every other potter of note throughout the Potteries. Among the names of those who made cream-ware we find John Turner, William Adams, Elijah Mayer, Warburton, Baddeley, and a host of lesser men whose products were nevertheless so uniformly good that in the usual absence of marks it is impossible to distinguish them from those made at Etruria.

Much Wedgwood cream-ware was left plain white, relying for its beauty on symmetry of form, good modelling and, above all, cut and pierced designs in silver style. The technique of piercing the soft, unfired clay with metal tools was similar to that used by the Chinese makers of 'rice-grain' ware and by the later Worcester artists, but Wedgwood speeded up the process, later, by using dies which cut a part or the whole of a pattern in a single operation, Another undecorated kind of cream-ware, tinted slightly blue, and appropriately stained with yellow or pink to imitate mother-o'-pearl, was called 'Pearl Ware', and was used to imitate sea-shells. The 'Queen's' and 'Pearl' bodies were used for domestic services of plain, good design, and for more fanciful, elaborately modelled tiered centre-pieces, cruets, vases, and other ornamental wares.

Figure 29. Wedgwood cream-ware.

When Wedgwood wished to decorate his ware it was obvious to him that printing afforded a ready means of producing domestic articles cheaply in large quantities. Accordingly he made use of the Liverpool workshops of Sadler and Green, who applied their black, puce or red transfers before returning the goods to have painted borders added. These borders are indeed characteristic of Wedgwood cream-ware decoration, featuring husk and key patterns, interlacing semicircles and scrolls, leaves, garlands, ribbons and geometrical patterns in brown, red, black and puce. It is a tribute to its makers that this simple kind of decoration looks as fresh now as it did the day it was applied.

Although Wedgwood had his own decorating shops, most of the enamelling was done outside the factory, notably by a Mrs Warburton's staff at Hot Lane (Cobridge), by a colony of porcelain painters in Chelsea and, almost certainly, by the two

Figure 30. Leeds cream-ware.

Cobridge Dutchmen who decorated salt-glazed wares. Best known of all painted cream-ware are specimens of a dinner and dessert service made for Catherine II of Russia, completed in 1774. It is said that the cost of the painting of British scenery (over twelve hundred different views) and floral and foliate borders accounted for £2,000 of the total cost of £5,000. So far as factory decoration is concerned, it is on record that a special palette of soft colours was evolved to suit the slightly yellowish ware.

Leeds cream-ware is quite as good as that made by Wedgwood, though it can be distinguished therefrom by greater lightness of

weight and a glaze which tends to show green in the crevices.
The best period was between 1783 (when the proprietors were
Hartley, Greens & Co.) and the end of the century, for though at
first the ware was imitative of Wedgwood's, the proprietors later
produced original designs outstanding for their lightness and
delicacy. To begin with, the pierced ware was always made with
separate dies, thus avoiding any sort of mechanical appearance.

Figure 31. Leeds cream-ware.

Piercing was used effectively to lighten the appearance of large
pieces such as candelabra and centre-pieces of which even the
bases were patterned, and so were the rims of dishes, plates and
trays. The Wedgwood borders were seldom used by the Leeds
designers, who preferred to outline gadrooned, foliated or
feather-moulded edges in blue.

A good deal of Leeds cream-ware is decorated in underglaze
blue in the Chinese style of Worcester and Bow, and the collector

learns to distinguish between the greenish lead glaze and the rather dirty blue glaze of similarly decorated Liverpool wares. Furthermore, a Leeds characteristic is the presence, on plates, of three spur-marks on the fronts and nine under the backs of the rims, made by the 'cockspurs' used to separate them during the firing.

Leeds coloured decoration runs the gamut of styles, oriental, flowers, ships, and scenes of rustic life, but a common feature is a panel of verse, usually moral or sentimental, enclosed within a frame of leaves or flowers. Many pieces are dated, and tea-pots and jugs commonly have twisted handles with applied flowers at the terminals. The colours used by the factory artists were green, lilac, buff and red, and pieces which show the use of a more ambitious palette were probably decorated elsewhere. It is known, for instance, that Leeds ware was bought 'in the white' by an artist named Allen, of Lowestoft, who added his own enamelling, mostly of coastal and shipping scenes, with occasional verses, before offering it for sale.

Other makers of cream-ware include Josiah Spode, David Dunderdale of Castleford, Greens, Bingley & Co. of Rockingham (who covered their ware with rich, brown glaze), and numerous potters at Newcastle and Sunderland, whose use of lustre pigments will be discussed in a later chapter.

CHAPTER SEVENTEEN

The Wedgwood school

JOSIAH WEDGWOOD, more than any other man, was responsible for the rise of the Potteries to worldwide renown towards the end of the eighteenth century. He allied business acumen to technical skill and inventive genius to a remarkable degree, and he never let slip an opportunity to adopt any style or process which he sensed was likely to meet with public approval. Naturally enough there were occasions when he laid himself open to the charge of being merely an imitator; on more than one occasion he was guilty of putting his material to quite unsuitable uses. Nevertheless, his love for all that was best in classical art and his insistence on perfection weigh heavily in the balance against accusations of that kind, and the name of Wedgwood and of his wares has always deserved and received a respect second to none among connoisseurs and collectors.

The cream-wares perfected by Wedgwood, and the kind of decoration he applied to them have been discussed, and attention can now be given to the other kinds of ware for which he is famous. First, without doubt, is his wonderful jasper, with which he was experimenting as early as 1773, and which was perfected two years later. It was a time when a revival of classicism was in the air, the time of the brothers Adam, of excavations at Herculaneum and Pompeii, and of inspiring translations of Homer's works into the English language. With this movement jasper wares were entirely in keeping.

The jasper body was a hard, finely-grained, semi-translucent stoneware containing sulphate of barium, and its pure whiteness could be stained with metallic oxides to produce blue, sage-green, olive-green, lilac-pink, yellow, or black. The whiteness, however, could be varied at will, and though on ordinary wares it is somewhat chalky, on finer pieces it may have the delicate hue of ivory or vellum. Similarly, though when necessary the body could be made opaque, it could alternatively be made so translucent that the ground colour appears in a slight degree through the thinner parts of the cameo reliefs, giving them a light, delicate texture. At first the body was stained right through, and is called 'solid jasper', but after about 1777 'jasper dip' was produced by staining only the surface of the ware, which in either form was capable of taking a very high polish. Occasionally the two kinds were used on one piece.

The usual two-coloured jasper bears applied, delicately stamped white ornaments, which were carefully undercut and trimmed, but three-coloured specimens, utilizing two colours of body with the white reliefs, are much rarer and so extremely valuable. Alternatively, the reliefs themselves could of course be stained any colour. Wedgwood's inspiration for the classical style of ornamentation he favoured came from engraved gems and classic reliefs, and he applied the result to ornamental vases and other pieces, sets of cameos representing famous men, ancient and modern, domestic wares, large plaques, and sets of smaller ones which were intended to be set in fireplaces and furniture. With Bentley as his faithful, enthusiastic disciple, he explored every avenue to find subjects worthy of reproduction, and employed a capable band of designers and artists which included John Flaxman, James Tassie, George Stubbs, William Hackwood and many others, both amateur and professional. Wedgwood himself considered his masterpiece to be the reproduction of the third-century Barberini Vase, lent to him by the Duke of Portland. This was made of a dark blue glass decorated with white glass cameos, for which Wedgwood substituted blue-black and white jasper. It was his intention to make fifty vases, but so far about twenty only are known, in various collections, although a new series was produced early in the nineteenth century, examples of which are fairly common. The collector has to remember that this 'Portland Vase', as it is more usually called, has been made in various sizes (the original was $10\frac{1}{4}$ in. high) and of various materials, not only by Wedgwoods, but also by his many imitators.

The quality of texture and colour of the jasper body lent itself admirably to the making of many miscellaneous objects, both decorative and utilitarian. The chess player probably covets a set of the chessmen designed by Flaxman in 1785, which sold at six guineas the set. The king, queen and bishop are particularly well modelled, in the medieval style, and the two sides were made in blue and white, black and white, and olive-green and lilac. Apart from tea- and coffee-sets made in all the various colours of both solid jasper and jasper-dip, still more beautiful ones were made with decoration in radiating stripes, with acanthus-leaf borders. Equally lovely are those tea-wares fashioned either entirely of white jasper, or else bearing reliefs in sage-green and lilac on the same, very rare body. Other unusual objects which can be found include pipe-bowls, hookah bowls for the eastern market, scent-bottles, handles for bell-pulls, chandeliers, ear-rings and mounts for opera-glasses.

Wedgwood's black basalt, which he called 'Egyptian black', was a rich black colour, smooth-surfaced, and a great improvement upon the superficially similar Elers body. It was used extensively for the making of services, but it is seen at its best in the form of ornamental pieces, and plaques modelled in high relief, when the absence of colours allows the eye the better to appreciate beauty of form and the play of light and shade. The material was ideal for the making of busts and statuettes, which were occasionally made to resemble bronze by the addition to the paste of metallic powder. Another treatment was painting in enamel colours, and relief decoration was occasionally added in red. The Elers red body was imitated by Wedgwood in his 'rosso antico', and he stained the same basic clay to produce chocolate, bamboo, cane and green wares which are given the name of 'terra-cotta'. They are usually decorated in relief, in contrasting colours of clay.

The Whieldon technique of making 'solid agate' ware was continued, and Wedgwood also used surface colouring on the cream-ware body, to give the same effect. His fine imitations of the natural agate were equalled by those of other stones, including porphyry and granites speckled with green, grey, black and white. These were all surface coloured on cream-ware, which was often left uncoloured as regards plinths, handles and rims. Gilding was sparingly used.

It should be noted that the desirable Wedgwood ware usually bears the impressed WEDGWOOD mark, whereas the presence of the word ENGLAND denotes a date after 1891, when it was added to comply with the regulations of the McKinley Tariff Act. Similarly, three capital letters (the first two workmen's marks, the third a date letter commencing A for the year 1840) convey a warning to those who wish to collect only the early ware.

It was to be expected that other potters should imitate wares whose popularity was due to Wedgwood's unerring sense of what the public wanted, and to his courage in putting it into large-scale production. His jasper, for example, had many imitators, chief of whom were John Turner and William Adams. The latter indeed was one of Josiah's greatest friends, and had actually worked with him. His jasper body was in fact every bit as good as Wedgwood's, but his blue rather tends towards violet, and his fame rests more upon his modelling skill, which enabled him to produce white relief designs of incomparable quality. As a master potter he worked at Greengates from 1789 onwards, and he made also cream-ware, stoneware and black basalts. Much of the blue-printed earthenware that was so popular some years ago was made by Adams, though it was a namesake working at Cobridge who first put the process into full operation, with the help of William Davies who left Worcester to join him in 1775. Adams (of Greengates) made stoneware goblets, mugs, jugs and loving-cups of fine quality, with glazed bands of darker brown around necks and bases, and decorated with sporting and drinking scenes in low relief.

John Turner began work at Lane End about 1762. His jaspers are not so good as Wedgwood's because his blue inclines too much to grey, but his white stoneware and black basalts are well-nigh perfect. His white stoneware jugs and mugs, very like those made by Adams, and sometimes mounted in silver or

Sheffield Plate, are most carefully decorated with clear-cut, detailed relief ornament, usually hunting scenes, and a feature often is the presence of bands of pale blue enamel around necks and rims. Much of his cream-ware, of excellent quality, was decorated in the Dutch style by outside enamellers.

There were many potters named Mayer, Mayers or Meir who made wares very similar to Wedgwood's. The white stoneware made by John, Joseph & Thomas Mayer of Dalehall is indistinguishable from his, and the same may be said of the black basalt, usually painted in the encaustic style, made by Elijah Mayer. At the same time none of these potters copied Wedgwood's styles, although the same cannot be said of Henry Palmer (later Palmer & Neale) who it is said worried Josiah by his duplication, in ware of equal excellence, of everything new that was evolved at Etruria.

The collector is in difficulties when he tries to attribute unmarked pieces of jasper, black basalt, white stoneware, or even cream-ware to one particular factory. Indeed, space here forbids the mention of more than a few of the very many men who belonged to what is known as 'The Wedgwood School'. In addition to those already mentioned, others were Samuel Hollins (maker of chocolate or red stoneware tea-pots and coffee-pots bearing gun-metal or silver lustre bands), Daniel Steel (blue jasper), Rogers, Lakin, F. Meir (fine blue-printed earthenware), Shorthose (black basalt) and Clews.

CHAPTER EIGHTEEN

Blue-printed earthenwares

THE introduction of transfer printing had a greater influence upon the development of the British ceramic industry than any other single factor. The process enabled decorated ware to be cheaply and easily produced, it helped semi-skilled decorators to reproduce faithfully the finest work of a single designer, and, above all, it brought that fine design within reach of everyone.

Printing in underglaze blue really began on porcelain, when the Worcester men adapted the overglaze process to imitate 'Blue Nankin', and when Thomas Turner invented the 'Willow Pattern' at Caughley. It must have been clear that the Chinese blue-painted porcelain, imported through the East India Company, provided an inexhaustible supply of patterns which could be used by anyone, but it was Turner who recognized the value of underglaze blue printing as a means of copying them in quantity. According to Jewitt 'every possible means seems to have been taken to secure secrecy', although as we have seen, the Caughley concern printed upon Worcester wares as well as upon its own. Turner, then, adapted Chinese landscapes and motifs, and invented his own patterns in the same style, including his 'Broseley Dragon' and 'Fisherman', as well as the 'Willow Pattern'.

It is very noticeable that practically all the early blue-printed patterns, wherever produced, have a crowded composition that is the absolute antithesis of the true Chinese instinct for reticent, economical design. No Chinaman could ever have perpetrated the 'willow pattern', and for the explanation of this apparent paradox we have to look to the Chinese rapidly increasing trade with the West. Europeans liked crowded, well-covered ware, and the Chinese obliged with styles of decoration which they would never have countenanced for their own use. These were the styles which the blue-printers copied, and even when new

116

ones were evolved, which owed nothing to eastern influence, they were still just as crowded.

The fashion set by Turner was quickly taken up by Josiah Spode, who in 1781 engaged Thomas Lucas, an engraver, and James Richards, a printer, both from Caughley, to found his own printing 'school'. To Stoke also, in 1789, went Thomas Minton, pupil of Turner, taking with him his own engraved plates, and many others made by his master. There were many

Figure 32. Spode 'willow pattern'.

early problems involved in the necessary translation of Chinese brush-strokes and colour-washes into engraved line. For instance, in order to make a Chinese mandarin 'stand out' clearly from the background it was necessary at first to burnish out a circular patch of white around him, while parallel lines, closely spaced or wide apart, had to take the place of colour-washes. The process itself was perfectly simple, the colour mixed with oil was worked into the engraved lines of a copper plate, and taken therefrom by means of the tissue-paper transfer. Great care had to be taken to ensure neat joints in the pattern, particularly in the case of borders, and of course every design had to be made in different sizes to suit different articles.

Inspired as they were by Chinese originals, the designs have an added interest that is due to the inventiveness of the English engravers, whose trees bear jewel-like fruits and whose pagodas become enchanted palaces. We are looking, of course, at a China which is far removed from actuality, but which is like what every European expected it to be, complete with snow-clad mountains, swirling torrents, mysterious temples and quite ridiculous bridges.

As time passed, and certainly by the end of the eighteenth century, blue-printed designs gradually lost their oriental appearance as more native styles were adopted. English scenery became popular, usually with cattle, views of famous mansions and estates, and Italian scenery, with ruins. For the Indian market there were hunting scenes with elephants, tigers and beaters, and copies of contemporary engravings, such as the 'Dr Syntax' series, were readily accepted. The American trade was not neglected, and we find sets of topographical views and famous personalities accompanied, as were most of the nine-teenth-century patterns, by floral or foliate borders, or by more elaborate ones featuring shells, scrolling, or portrait, animal or landscape vignettes.

The blue used was the usual cobalt blue used always for underglaze work, which gave different tones according to its purity. Whereas on early porcelain the blue may be almost indigo or grey, the earthenware printers were sufficiently masters of their material to be able at will to produce clear light or dark blues, or even the near violet which had been introduced at Caughley by Turner. It was a question of fashion, for at first a light blue was preferred, to give place, about 1800, to a dark blue which was again ousted by the lighter colour some thirty years later.

Many of the finer English, French and American landscape prints were engraved between 1818 and 1846 by the firm of Enoch Wood & Sons, and can be dated with fair accuracy by means of the borders used with them. Sea-shell and floral motifs were followed about 1830 by oak-leaves, vine motifs and berries, or by floral arrangements interrupted by six scrolled reserves, outside an intertwining ribbon. The American views, suddenly popular as a result of the outcome of the war, were best produced by William Adams & Co. and by Ralph Stevenson of Cobridge, whose borders of hawthorn and vine, acorns and oak-leaves, and scrolls and flowers are particularly well designed. The 'Dr Syntax' series previously mentioned, after the famous Rowlandson prints, was produced by James and Ralph Clews, who were responsible also for an equally fine set of Don Quixote's adventures.

CHAPTER NINETEEN

Lustre wares

THE decoration of earthenware by means of metallic salts of
gold and platinum was originally an attempt to imitate the
appearance of vessels made of precious metals. So far as surface resemblance was concerned the attempt was successful,
but the comparative clumsiness of even the best earthenwares
prevented the exact copying of, say, a silver cream jug or tea-pot,
and lustre is best recognized for what it really is, an attractive
kind of decoration when used in conjunction with moulding,
painting or printing. Furthermore, lustred ware is seen at its
best in a cottage rather than in a drawing-room; it looks better
upon a set of dresser shelves than in a cabinet.

Silver lustre, perhaps the most successful of all, was obtained
from the platinum salts, a range of tones from copper to bronze
and gold from salts of gold, and the same gold salts were
used to produce a range of pinks and purples. These chemical
processes were understood and used in the Near East as early as
the ninth century, and the art spread thence to Spain, where in
the fourteenth, fifteenth and sixteenth centuries the splendid
Hispano-Moresque wares were made by Moorish potters. In the
early eighteenth century, about 1715, Böttger discovered the
preparation of a purplish lustre, derived from gold, which was
used on Meissen porcelain, and in this country Josiah Wedgwood
used lustres made from gold salts some time before 1780, while
his son Thomas introduced silver lustre about ten years later.

Our earliest lustre wares, therefore, were made by the Wedgwoods, and survive in the form of the rare shell pieces, made of
'Pearl Ware', whose pinkish colour was in fact a lustre. Such
pieces are rare, and it is safe to say that most of the lustre ware
which is nowadays collected was made during the nineteenth
century, notably in Staffordshire, but also at Bristol, Swansea,
Leeds, Sunderland and Newcastle. Also, it is perhaps well to

mention at this juncture that the market is flooded with modern reproductions of silver-resist and Sunderland wares (to be discussed later) which are betrayed by an obvious bright, unrubbed lustre, and a white body which shows none of the signs of age or use. In fact, genuine old lustre is very easily worn away by constant use, or by washing in hot water.

Copper lustre is commoner than any other, and it varies a great deal both in quality and in colour. The latter depends not only on the kind of salt used, but also on the kind of clay beneath

Figure 33. Wedgwood pearl ware.

it, and we find every tone of copper, bronze and gold, even of brown when the lustre has worn thin. The best copper lustre, applied to thinly potted ware, has an extremely smooth surface, especially inside the foot-rim where it has not been scratched, with no grittiness or irregularity, a defect which often betrays a reproduction. The poorest variety has no other decoration of any kind, and its monotonous appearance is at once relieved when, as is common, bands of yellowish buff, simply patterned in lustre, are placed upon it. Another common kind of decoration was done by 'masking' bands or panels from the lustre, resulting in white surfaces which could then be filled in with enamel painting, transfer-printing (usually in pink on Swansea wares), or pink lustre, either plain or attractively mottled. Some pieces bear decoration painted directly on the lustred surface, usually in red, green and blue, or on such moulded reliefs as vine patterns, hunting scenes or garden flowers, and a type of jug usually associated with Wales features moulded panels or vertical stripes which are lustred, leaving the rest of the body white or washed over with thin enamel.

Silver lustre was extensively used for the making of tea-pots, cream jugs, slop-basins and vases of all kinds, as the poor man's

Figure 34. Silver resist.

substitute for silver. We find many pieces upon which it was used instead of gilding, it is found in broad bands around the rims and bases of black-printed jugs, and it sometimes 'frames' enamelled decoration. Commonly, the body of pieces so decorated was left white, but more rarely it was painted yellow or blue, and such pieces are valuable. The same observation holds good of 'resist' wares. This is the name given to the result of a process in which the decoration, animals, birds, flowers and leaves, agricultural implements and so on, was painted in a soluble solution. After dipping this was washed away, leaving the design unlustred and clearly defined. Alternatively, of course, the design itself could alone receive the lustre. Occasionally silver-resist wares were further sparingly decorated with enamels.

Apart from the use of gold lustre in bands upon copper lustre, and in thin washes inside silver-lustred articles, it is usually found in mottled or marbled washes on a class of ware credited to Sunderland, consisting mostly of jugs (some of them very large), bowls and mugs, bearing doggerel verses and black-printed representations of the Wear Bridge, shipping, mariner's compass, harvest scenes and masonic emblems.The same printed ornament, which is often washed in carelessly with crude enamels, is to be found upon the purple-lustred Sunderland wall-plaques, which alternatively may bear religious texts. Most of these are rectangular in shape, but oval and round ones are also known. Their sombre nature is sometimes relieved by dainty little sprays of enamelled flowers. The presence of pink (gold) lustre in little blobs or 'squiggles' is very common on many Staffordshire wares, such as moulded stirrup-cups in the shape of fox masks, and cottage jugs of a type usually credited to the Aynsley pottery, decorated in crude india-red and blue. There is also a very common type of Staffordshire tea and dinner service, made of fine quality porcelain with a white translucency, which is decorated in very much the same way, with the additional colour of a good bright yellow.

The use of lustre has never been discontinued, though it is not always recognized as such. Later examples include the nacreous lustre which was used on Irish Belleek porcelain, and that used at Worcester in the mid-nineteenth century, both of which were produced from bismuth nitrate.

CHAPTER TWENTY

Swansea earthenware

SWANSEA is well known for its incomparable porcelain, but it is not generally known that it was the home of practically every kind of earthenware that was in vogue between about 1770 and 1870. The Swansea Pottery was actually founded in 1764 by William Coles, an iron-founder, who died about 1778, leaving it to his three sons, one of whom, John, apparently took the lead in producing ordinary red-glazed ware suitable for local farm use, a lead-glazed greyish earthenware, and cream-ware. In many ways, with the exception of the cream-ware, these products were throw-backs to the old medieval wares, for the decoration upon them consisted for the most part of crude incised patterns, and it was not until about 1786 that a certain George Haynes joined the firm to enlarge its premises, rename them the 'Cambrian Pottery', and begin the making of earthenware in the new style of Wedgwood.

The quality of the ware made at that time, just before the close of the century, can be anticipated when we consider some of the workmen employed at the reorganized factory. The Swansea porcelain painter, Thomas Pardoe, assisted by Evan Evans, decorated earthenware and cream-ware with landscapes, figures, birds, animals and flowers. Much fine underglaze blue printing was done from the engraved copper plates of Thomas Rothwell, including a series of local views, and George Bentley, working between about 1790 and 1798, was responsible for the modelling of figures, of which a recumbent Anthony and a companion Cleopatra, in black basalt or in yellow-glazed earthenware, are best known.

The Swansea (or Cambrian) wares of this period compare favourably with, and closely resemble those made in the Potteries, and they are often mistaken for them, if unmarked. There is simply no way of distinguishing between them. Ornamental pieces, particularly vases, candlesticks and lamps, as well as domestic wares are known to have been made in cream-ware, white earthenware, black basalt and cream-ware. The domestic ware is usually well-designed and potted, light in weight, and covered with a distinctive blued glaze. Much use was made of blue-printing as well as painting in blue, and we find more rarely overglaze printing in manganese purple, brown, and a greenish

Figure 35. Blue-painted plate of Swansea pottery.

black. The edges of 'flat ware' (plates and dishes) were sometimes painted in chocolate or orange.

A very important change in ownership came about when, in 1801, William Dillwyn purchased the lease of the factory, and a controlling interest in its working, on behalf of his son, Lewis Weston Dillwyn. Haynes remained as manager, and the firm was renamed Haynes, Dillwyn & Co., though the Dillwyns wisely restrained their activities to providing necessary extra capital and, probably, a certain better social standing which encouraged the patronage of such notabilities as Lord Nelson, and Sir

William and Lady Hamilton, who visited the factory in 1802. A new artist was engaged, named William Weston Young, to paint upon the improved cream-ware which was called 'Opaque China'. He was apparently expert at painting animals, butter-flies and birds, but it is Pardoe's brushwork that is more often seen upon this slightly yellow ware, mostly in the form of exact copies of the botanical plates in Curtis's *Botanical Magazine*. Transfer-printing was always used, and is seen at its best in some very dainty renderings of birds and shells, though at the other extreme nothing could be more incongruous than the 'willow pattern' and other designs that were sometimes applied to the bodies of the cow cream jugs that were made in large numbers.

A greal deal of lustre ware is to be found in South Wales, mostly in the form of jugs, but it differs in no way from that made in the Potteries and elsewhere, so that it would be unwise to say that it was all made in Swansea, in spite of what every proud cottager would say, At the same time it is known that from the very beginning the process was in use, in every known form, and it is therefore probable that their claims may some-times be well founded. It is possible that the jugs bearing vertical moulded ribs, and those which are decorated with panels of pink transferred decoration are the most likely to have been made at the factory.

The Dillwyns severed their connexion with Swansea in 1850, and one of their last efforts to bring about a revival of its failing fortunes was the introduction, about 1847, of a ware much resembling Wedgwood's encaustic decorated black basalt. It was made from red clay, from the Penllergaer estate, and the vases and other ornamental items were printed in black outline with classical subjects, which were then washed in with black enamel.

Another Welsh pottery working in Swansea between about 1813 and 1839 was known as the Glamorgan Pottery. It was founded by George Haynes, with his son-in-law William Baker, and its products were therefore very like those made by the larger rival concern. So far as we know very little original work was attempted, but the transfer printing was of a high standard, in blue and black particularly, and in the form of outlines which were washed in with bright enamels, just as they were at Spodes. The fact that both the Glamorgan and the Cambrian wares commonly bear impressed marks makes identification fairly straightforward, though this observation does not apply to lustred pieces.

The third pottery which must be mentioned, and which perhaps should have been included in a previous chapter, was established by a colony of Dutch potters, early in the seventeenth century, at Loughor, near to Swansea. They made a very distinctive kind of delft, a very heavy, clumsy ware that is quite unlike that which was made elsewhere. It is usually covered by a pale, yellow-green enamel, and bears carelessly drawn Chinese landscapes in bright green, manganese purple and grey. A characteristic feature is the almost invariable presence of silhouettes of birds somewhere in the border design, which takes the usual form of concentric circles, applied quickly on the decorator's turntable.

CHAPTER TWENTY-ONE

Pottery figures

IT is difficult to put into words the attraction which early earthenware figures have for so many collectors, and to explain why they should possess a value that seems, at first thought, to be out of proportion to their quality, both as regards their modelling and their decoration. True, some of them may be nearly two hundred and fifty years old, but age of itself guarantees neither aesthetic nor monetary worth. They were made for the most part by potters who had little or no modelling training or skill, and since they were made to sell for a few pence at country fairs or at the cottage door by pedlars or wandering potters, their decoration was of the simplest, slap-dash kind. Why, then, are they so admired? And why can a horseman mounted upon a Noah's Ark charger that a child might have modelled, be worth four figures in pounds?

In the first place, perhaps, we ought to draw a distinction between porcelain figures made at Meissen, Bow and Chelsea and these pottery images that at first, at any rate, had no sort of relationship to them. The former were made for polite society. Their place was on the dining-table or in the boudoir or drawing-room, they were designed and made by trained artists and craftsmen, and the painting upon them was of such quality that they could live unashamedly with the best that Chippendale, Hepplewhite or Sheraton could design. They were sophisticated. If their intent was to be humorous, it was a genteel, polite humour, and every beau or lady of fashion might see each other's counterpart, in exquisite miniature, ogling or simpering at them from the mantelpiece.

Just as a porcelain figure of this kind personified the kind of idyllic society that was beloved of Watteau and Fragonard, so does an earthenware one typify the commonly accepted idea of eighteenth-century rustic England, with its incurable sentimentality, its piety, its reverence for its betters, its love of out-door sport, and a sense of humour that was pithy, downright and often coarse. There, it might seem, lies the attraction. We see in pottery figures a reflection of what we like to think is our own national character, while at the same time we sympathize with their crudity, allied as it so often is to subdued, mellow colour and glistening lead glaze.

The earliest English figures, if they may be so called, are medieval, and take such forms as, perhaps, a drinking vessel in the shape of some abbot whose monastery had sheltered or given employment to an itinerant potter. Then there is a long gap until about 1670, when pieces seldom found outside museums were made of salt-glazed stoneware. It was John Dwight of Fulham whose workshops provided the first considerable flow of English ceramic sculpture, a series of grey or bronze-coloured statuettes and busts which some have attributed, so far as design is concerned, to the famous carver Grinling Gibbons. Certainly such well-known specimens as 'Lydia Dwight', 'Flora' and 'Prince Rupert' feature such sharp, incisive detail that there is good reason for such an attribution.

The period of Staffordshire salt-glazed figures extends roughly between 1730 and 1760. The earliest were of simple, rounded form, with spherical heads and stylized features, the eyes (and the buttons of costume) emphasized with blobs of dark clay. The well-known bell-shaped women are typical of the class, the flared skirt and bodice turned in the lathe, and the arms mere bent lengths of clay, with no attempt at modelling true to life. Apart from the use of contrasting darker blobs and stripes of colour, ornament is confined to whatever incised design could be applied in the lathe or by the potter's fingers, in contrast with the shredded clay which gives a characteristic appearance to the owl and bear-baiting jugs which were made in Staffordshire and at Nottingham.

Among the more ambitious salt-glazed sculpture are agate-ware cats and other animals in which the layers of clay were sometimes manipulated to suggest natural markings and, finest of all, the so-called 'Pew Groups'. These are found in several forms, and all are drolly humorous and sentimental. The two lovers were featured in many ways, as Adam and Eve on either side of a tree, complete with serpent, separated by a dog or a flask of wine, sometimes aloof and sometimes loving. On these finer pieces much more attention was paid to detail, and we find more colour in the shape of splashes of cobalt blue, and jewel-like enamels in bright pink, yellow and turquoise. Horsemen were modelled in a stylized, restrained way, very similar in style to those which belong to the next class we will go on to consider, the lead-glazed earthenware figures of the Astbury-Whieldon school.

John Astbury (1688–1743) is traditionally associated with earthenware figures made of coloured clay decorated with white, and covered by a clear, translucent lead glaze. But, because the work of another potter, Thomas Whieldon (1719–1795) is so like his (and doubtless like that of many other potters whose work and names are unrecorded) it is nowadays customary to classify figures of the period as Astbury-Whieldon. At the same time, whereas Astbury pieces usually have the blobbed eyes of the salt-glazed figures, those credited to Whieldon feature the use of coloured glazes in green, purple-brown, cobalt and rust-red. There is therefore a distinction, which is, however, seldom clear-cut enough to justify a definite attribution to either potter. Notable exceptions are the Astbury figures of musicians, on foot, seated, or mounted, pairs of lovers, seated men reading or drinking, and soldiers.

The technique of using coloured glazes of beautifully mellow yet glowing quality was carried further by Ralph Wood (1715–1772). For the first time, moreover, figures were modelled with care, the faces full of character, and costumes detailed. Humour was still to the fore, as typified by the cynical drinking-group, the 'Vicar and Moses', reeling home together, and a range of upwards of a hundred and sixty-five figures and groups includes classical subjects (Apollo, Neptune, Jove, Bacchus), sporting types (Gamekeeper, Sportsman), religious subjects (various

Apostles, King David, Lost Piece, Lost Sheep), sentimental subjects (Girl with Bird, Old Age, Peasant Worshipping, Tenderness, Friendship), notabilities (Voltaire, Van Tromp, Dr Franklin), animals and many types of countrymen and artisans. In fact, no kind of figure that might have appealed to simple rustic taste was neglected. The finest moulds in which such pieces were cast were made from blocks designed by, among others, Enoch Wood,

Figure 36. Astbury musician.

Ralph's nephew, and a Frenchman named John Voyez. Voyez worked for Wedgwood until discharged for drunkenness and alleged indecency, and he probably began to work for Wood about 1780. The figures credited to him, among them a fine jug known as 'Fair Hebe' and a splendid 'Hudibras', were either in classical style or else adapted from the works of Cyfflé, and their faces all have characteristic soft expressions, with rather protruding eyes and thick lips. Many Ralph Wood figures were left white, a creamy or a bluish-white, and since the details of the modelling are in that case unobscured by thick glaze, they show to much better advantage.

The finest of all Toby Jugs were made by Ralph Wood, the direct descendants of medieval vessels with human masks as lips, and of the Rhenish 'Bellarmines'. The Wood Toby, however, is purely English, and it has enjoyed a popularity that has never entirely waned. There are many distinct types, all of them very carefully modelled, with every small detail of face, hands and costume clear-cut and at times caricatured, and including the 'Thin Man', 'Lord Howe' (or the 'Sailor'), 'Squire', 'Fiddler', 'Planter', 'Bluff King Hal', 'Snuff Taker', 'Parson', and 'Martha Gunn'. Many models were made in both large and 'miniature' size. These Tobies, and of course the figures, are best when the coloured glazes of green, aubergine, grey, yellow, blue and brown are most subdued, carefully placed, but at the same time merging streakily into each other. It is most interesting to think that nowadays they are impossible to reproduce.

Ralph Wood's son, or Ralph Wood Junior as he is usually known, continued his father's range of figures and Toby Jugs, with the notable difference that he began to use overglaze enamels with, or instead of, coloured glazes. Their comparatively muddy appearance, showing brush-marks, is a fairly sure guide to their later origin. The third member of the Wood family, Enoch, made well-modelled figures, some of them of large size and including portrait busts such as his well-known one of Wesley. Despite their technical excellence, they are lifeless, stiff and ungainly compared with those made by the two Ralphs, a feature which is even more apparent in his later wares, made after he had entered into partnership with James Caldwell in 1790.

We seldom associate the name of Wedgwood with Staffordshire figures, and yet his name is often found impressed upon models usually credited to the Woods. This is not proof that he actually made them, however, for it is known that they supplied him with certain figures, such as the 'Madonna and Child', upon which he may have placed his mark. Alternatively, there is the possibility that other potters, jealous of Wedgwood's reputation, or wishing to trade upon his name, may have forged his mark. Apart from such doubtful pieces, Wedgwood did of course make busts and figures in white jasper and black basalt, in the neo-classic style. They are beautifully modelled, but they are nevertheless not in the true Staffordshire tradition. The very materials of which they were made puts them rather into the class of marble statuary, as distinctive from ceramic modelling.

A considerable class of figures is credited to James Neale, working with Humphrey Palmer at the latter end of the century, They have been described as 'chaste, dignified and decorous', and certainly they have an appearance, a pleasant Jane Austenish primness and delicacy which is more usually associated with porcelain. The reason, perhaps, is that Neale was a Londoner. and a cultured man. His models are usually small, commonly mounted upon elaborately moulded rectangular bases finished with a coloured line in pink, red or purple. Their costumes are usually finished with dainty sprigs and dots.

Among the potters who continued the Wood tradition at the turn of the century was John Walton, the founder of a school of figure makers such as Charles Tittensor, Obadiah Sherratt, Ralph Hall and Ralph Salt. We might almost call it the 'bocage school', because a feature of his models was the presence of an elaborate bocage of foliage as a background, in the style of Chelsea, which of course provided the inspiration. Nevertheless, the figures themselves were not copied from porcelain models, being in the main patriotic, sentimental, pious, and depictive of rustic life. At first he used coloured glazes, but upon his later wares, and particularly upon his large groups of 'Bull Baiting', 'Cows and Calves', 'Birds Nesting', 'Tithe Pig' and so on, he used strong enamels in apple-green, blue-green, red-brown, russet, blue, primrose and grey. His red-browns, pinks and blues were often dappled by means of short, wide brush-strokes. A characteristic feature of the bocage which is found upon this kind of 'poor man's porcelain' is the repetition of a branch or branches symmetrically arranged, each ending in five or six serrated leaves, radiating from a six-petalled flower, brightly coloured pink, blue, white or yellow. Most Walton figures and groups are clearly marked with his name impressed within a white, scrolled reverse, usually at the back of the model at the base of the bocage. The brothers Ralph and Charles Salt made almost identical models, though usually not so well modelled, John and Ralph Hall figures are even cruder though usually

Figure 37. Bull-baiting group.

decorated with charming sprig patterns, and Obadiah Sherratt is associated with representations of the crueller side of rural life. His large bull-baiting groups, such as the named 'Bull Baiting' and 'Now Captin Lad' spare nothing of every detail of brutality and they, like his other large models, are often mounted upon elaborate four- or six-legged table bases.

The Tittensor family carried on the Walton tradition well into the nineteenth century. Rarely marked pieces have the familiar bocage, and other identifying features are the two cherubs which often appear as supporters of urns or square tablets, and the contemporary costume (of the period about 1820) of the rather stiff, self-conscious countrymen and women which Charles, in particular, liked to portray.

The Pratt type of figure was made between about 1790 and 1820, decorated with underglaze, high-temperature colours of purple-brown, pale yellow, grey-brown, muddy blue, olive-green and thick orange of the kind usually associated with Felix Pratt of Felton. Their modelling is crude enough to suggest an earlier date, and the decoration, commonly in the form of large and small spots is most distinctive.

We now come to the kind of figure known as the 'Victorian Chimney Ornament' which is best represented by the familiar 'china dog', with a chain around his neck, who stands patiently on either side of a cottage fireplace just as his ancestor, the Chinese 'Dog of Fo', stood on either side of the gates of some Buddhist temple. This class of ornament, usually made in a three-part mould, is sparing of decoration, it stands usually upon a smooth, flattened oval base, and it has a flat back, not only because it was meant to stand on a mantelpiece, but also because modelling (and cost) were so greatly eased. Practically every model, apart from the dogs, features the abundant use of a very intense, lustrous dark blue, together with red, green and purplish pink. We often see quite elaborate tartan or chintz patterning, and many pieces have their titles on the fronts of their bases, picked out in enamel or gold. Indeed, this was often necessary, because the same moulds were sometimes used for more than one figure. As time went on the colouring became more sparse, being often confined to flesh tints for faces and hands, black for the hair, and gold.

It has often been suggested that these chimney ornaments comprise a pictorial history of the social life and interests of Victorian Britain. Certainly the range was very wide. Sport is well represented by such figures as 'Tom Cribb', 'Fred Archer' and 'George Parr'. The popularity of the circus was responsible for many groups and figures of elephants, horses, harlequins, performing dogs and bears, showmen and showwomen. Crime, religion, popular notabilities, and nationalism—all these were represented, and in addition there is a host of cottages, churches, castles, and buildings connected with some crime or other event of popular interest. As to who made them (and upwards of two hundred are recorded by name), one can say only that of the many potters who must have profited by an obvious demand, Sampson Smith is best known. He was born in 1813, died in 1878, and appears to have begun his work in Longton in 1846. His activities in this regard are proved by the fact that some of his original block moulds were discovered in a derelict part of the factory in which he worked.

CHAPTER TWENTY-TWO

Other earthenwares

In the previous chapters an attempt has been made to classify our earthenwares according to the kind of body and glaze which was in fashion during various periods. At the same time, however, it is clear that such a broad classification has necessarily not embraced many kinds of ware which do not readily lend themselves to it. Likewise, the names of many quite well-known potteries have been omitted.

At the risk of repetition, the many important attempts at earthenware or stoneware making by Spodes claim attention. Josiah Spode the First, though at times an opportunist in plagiarism, made no slavish copies of Wedgwood's black basalts, red wares, and jaspers, but nevertheless he made domestic wares of all three bodies, breaking away from classicism because as a stolid Englishman he disliked it. When he used a classical motif he usually made it subsidiary to coloured scrolling, or floral and foliate wreaths and sprays. His stoneware jugs and mugs have none of the classicism, say, of those made by Hollins. They closely resemble those made by Turner, featuring the hunting and rustic scenes beloved also by Davenport. Indeed, Spode stoneware is as it were a mirror held to the tradition of the 'fine old English Gentleman' of mid-eighteenth-century squirearchy. To Josiah reliefs featuring English subjects were much more appealing than those which dragged foreign gods and goddesses from their dusty obscurity. Strangely enough, as we have already seen, he loved anything Chinese, and many of his stoneware models, with Chinese subjects in relief, show a marked allegiance to the Elers tradition, though even then he could not always resist the inclusion of the tendrils, leaves and fruit of the vine in the decorative scheme.

Josiah Spode the Second inherited his father's love of Chinese design, and when the hard, fine white earthenware called 'Stone China' was introduced in 1805 he lost no time in decorating it with the same kind of patterns, in bright colour, that had hitherto been rendered in transfer-printed underglaze blue. This he did by using the process of outline printing that had long been a Spode speciality, and which has since become the basis of all modern decoration, not only of domestic ware, but also of ornamental pieces the cost of which, under present-day conditions, would otherwise be prohibitive. Quite briefly, any set pattern was outlined by means of transfer in blue, black, biscuit-brown or chestnut-brown. Coloured enamel and gold were then added according to the wishes of the designer. Ground colours might be used, plain or stippled, and flowers, leaves, birds and other motifs painted in many different combinations of colour. Sometimes transferred shapes were left quite white. There was no end to this sort of permutation of design, its character could vary according to the head designer's will, or alternatively a dozen artists, given a free hand, could produce a dozen different colour arrangements.

Spodes were not the only potters who made a strong earthenware for domestic use, that was at the same time very like porcelain in appearance. Mintons produced their 'Amherst Japan' series in a very similar body, and so did Davenports, Alcocks of Cobridge, Hicks, Johnson and Meigh, giving it such names as 'Royal Ironstone China', 'Warranted Ironstone China', 'Semi-China', 'Royal Semi-Porcelain' and so on, but it was left to the firm of C. J. Mason & Co. to make the best-known ware of all, the 'Mason's Ironstone China' that was first introduced in 1813. This body contained no ironstone (slag) at all, but its name indicated its tough, extremely strong, heavy nature. It was used to make domestic services, ornamental vases up to about four feet in height, and even fireplaces and mantelpieces. It is clear that from the start the intention was to provide a substitute for valuable Chinese porcelain, for those who could not afford to buy it but who wished, as we would say, to 'keep up with the Joneses'. Mason therefore copied the most colourful Chinese styles, using the Spode method of transferred outline, with results that are usually overpowering, but occasionally very close in appearance to the Chinese originals. The ware itself was slightly blued, again in imitation of the Chinese paste. We sometimes find an occasional piece decorated with fruit, flowers or landscapes, either painted delicately with a brush or else washed in over a transferred outline. One of the really lovely Mason designs, rarely seen, features flower sprays, some painted and some in fine gold, scattered over the surface of the ware. A ground colour much favoured was a rather muddy lavender, and a common style features flowers and butterflies in gold, or enamelled, upon an intense, lustrous, translucent dark blue ground.

The ornamental vases made by Masons were naturally copied from the oriental, with handles elaborately scrolled or modelled in the forms of dragons and other mystical beasts. Jugs were made in the familiar hexagonal shape, in various sizes, and these and other pieces, such as mugs, commonly have dragon or snake handles which are crudely scaled in green and rust-red. The factory closed down in 1851, but the same ware was continued by Ashworths, and is still made at the present day. The collector has to remember that the same printed mark has always been used, and to look for the earlier impressed mark, or for the signs of wear and age upon any piece he wishes to acquire.

The practice of supplying a cheaper imitation of a fashionable but expensive ware has always been common and, to the collector, extremely dangerous. A very fine, light earthenware was made by Booths of Tunstall towards the end of the nineteenth century, to be decorated with the most easily recognizable Worcester patterns, in particular the 'exotic birds' reserved on a scale-blue ground and the underglaze blue-printed 'pine-cone' pattern. The cobalt blue used was exactly the right shade, and the enamelling leaves little to be desired. We find well-potted baskets with pierced sides, with or without handles, very fine vases and domestic wares, all of the correct Worcester shape, but the lightness of weight and the complete opacity are sufficient safeguards against mistaking 'Booths' for the true Worcester.

Many potters, notably of the same late nineteenth- and early twentieth-century period, have copied the colourful monochrome and flambé wares of the East. William de Morgan had a pottery at Fulham from about 1870, and as an artist-potter he aimed high by imitating the intense purples and blues, and the lustres of Persian ware. Some of his patterns are quite modern in conception, marked by strong, flowing line and a fine sense of composition. At Jackfield in Shropshire, the home of much earlier black-glazed red ware 'sprigged' in the Astbury style, the firm of Craven, Dunnill & Co. made a very similar contemporary lustred ware. Their large plaques, made of buff-coloured clay and decorated in purple and red lustrous enamels, highly iridescent, are typical products of the William Morris school. The earlier Jackfield ware referred to is often mistaken for Astbury or Whieldon, so much so that it has been suggested that the Jackfield potters may have bought either their moulds or the ware itself from Burslem. However that may be, Jackfield ware may often be recognized by the presence thereupon of traces of unfired oil gilding and oil-colours, though an occasional piece may bear enamelled decoration, usually in the shape of flowers.

The popularity of the 'pot-lids' printed by Felix Pratt of Fenton has never waned. They, together with every kind of domestic ware, dessert services, toilet sets, and mugs were decorated by the process of underglaze printing in colours that was perfected by Pratt in time for the Great Exhibition of 1851. These colours, which had gradually been developed to resist a high kiln temperature, most of them from about 1800 onwards, include orange (from litharge and antimony), chrome-green, rose-pink, blue-green, purple-brown (from manganese), cobalt-blue, black and brown. The amazing feature of the Pratt prints is that each colour was applied from a separate transfer, and yet the registration is always perfect.

Another kind of Pratt ware made between about 1780 and 1820 comprises tea-pots, jugs, flasks and plaques which have moulding in the forms of acanthus and oak leaves, ears of corn, twisted ribbons and relief representation of notabilities (Lord Jervis, Nelson, Wellington, etc.) and sentimental subjects

(Sailor's Farewell and Return, Innocence, Mischief, etc.). The decoration of these pieces was carried out in crude but fresh-looking high-temperature colours of yellow, green, red and blue, the same colours in fact that were used on Pratt figures. Some of the tea-pots, oval in section with vertical sides, the lid fitting snugly within a gallery, are very similar to those made at Castleford during the same period. The latter, however, were made of

Figure 38. Pratt moulded jug.

fine stoneware, seldom have any decoration apart from the moulding, and often have their edges outlined in blue enamel.

The typical brown glaze of Rockingham is seen to best advantage on the heavily potted earthenware made between about 1796 and 1806. It is smooth, highly lustrous, and attractively uneven in tone. Apart from its use upon Toby Jugs, flasks in various forms (pistols and boots are best-known) and frog-mugs, we often see it on 'Cadogan' tea-pots. These strange articles, made also by Mintons and copied from a form of Chinese wine-pot, are in the shape of a peach, without a lid, and filled through a hole in the base, on the principle of a non-spillable ink-pot.

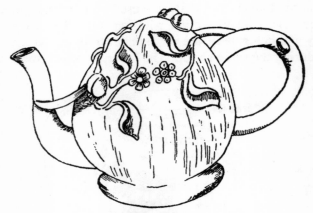

Figure 39. Rockingham 'cadogan'.

CHAPTER TWENTY-THREE

The identification of pottery and porcelain

EVERY collector likes to be able to identify his specimens. He may even hope (and sometimes his hope may be realized) that he may one day recognize a treasure by virtue of his superior knowledge, lying unrecognized in an antique shop. Such happy events are certainly not unknown, for not every dealer is a specialist.

But even putting this consideration to one side, knowledge is a pleasant thing to have, and anyone making a collection should not be entirely at the mercy of the vendor, however honest he may be. It is always safe to buy from a reputable specialist, but there is much satisfaction in being able to purchase on the strength of one's own opinion, rather than to shelter behind a cheque-book.

Of course, this kind of knowledge does not come easily or quickly. The connoisseur has handled so many pieces that he recognizes the identity of a piece almost by instinct. And this instinct, for want of a better word, is really the immediate observation of many different characteristics which together lead to a conclusion. It follows therefore that it ought to be possible to suggest a procedure which, though at first laborious, may with practice and in the course of time become 'instinctive'.

Take up the piece in your hands. Is it porcelain or earthenware? Hold it against a very strong light. (I always keep at hand a box containing a powerful electric bulb, which is allowed to shine through a two-inch hole.) If light shines through the piece, it is probably porcelain, though this is not certain. Some stonewares, if thinly potted, will allow a little light to penetrate, and much Bow porcelain is completely opaque, even at the edges and in the centre of the base where the body is often thinnest.

Suppose that the piece is quite opaque, that the decoration upon it is unlike anything that was done at Bow, and that it therefore seems to be made of earthenware. What kind of earthenware? A lead glaze is unmistakably smooth and glossy, a tin glaze white, more or less blued, even a little pink, and perhaps a little chipped at the edges to show the clay beneath. But then, delft painting is so very bold. Is it salt-glazed? A little experience will enable you to recognize the slightly pitted surface, more or less pronounced. Very soon a decision will be reached, but there is still a long way to go, and all the time the kind of information you have tried to absorb in the previous chapters of this book is running through your mind—the different enamels and lustres, the difference between painting and printing, the unmistakable decoration of Pratt pot-lids, and so on. You will quickly decide what variety of earthenware you have in your hands—and which, let us hope, you are not holding by its handle—and all that remains is the question of its provenance. That is not so easy. One clay looks very like another. Only experience can tell you whether you are looking at a character-istic shape or pattern. Perhaps, though, a mark may help? On a piece of earthenware it probably will, for marks were seldom if ever forged. And as you put the piece down upon the table you realize that its unusual weight or its lightness, its potting thin or thick, has helped you to come to a decision through your sense of touch.

Suppose, now, that some degree of light shines through the piece, and that it is not salt-glazed stoneware. Apparently it is porcelain. Is it then English or foreign? Is it made of 'soft-paste' or 'hard-paste'? And if the latter, was it made in the Far East or on the Continent, or at one of our own 'hard-paste' factories? Despite all that has been said or written, it is not easy to dis-tinguish between the two kinds of paste. Some English artificial pastes, such as the later Worcester ones, are nearly as hard as true pastes, that is they were baked in a 'hard' or high-temperature fire, and are also hard to the touch. There are many tests. A hard-paste does not warm so quickly to the touch, it will resist a sharp point or a file, a fracture will be glassy, not rough or granulated. A hard-paste may be disfigured by tiny pits, often blackened, in the glaze, but a soft-paste may bear traces of sand, and its glaze may be clouded with tiny black specks, or tiny bubbles that are clearly seen under a magnifying glass.

The glaze protecting a soft-paste is usually (though not always) itself soft, and it may be scratched or even completely worn away in places where it has received the most wear. The decoration in the bottom of an early Worcester or Lowestoft bowl, for instance, may be almost entirely missing. The glaze on a hard-paste was fired with it, and became a part of it, but the thickness of a soft glaze can often be clearly estimated, like the glass in a picture-frame. Similarly, enamels have sunk into the glaze and body of a piece of soft-paste, while those upon a true porcelain tend to stand out in low relief.

So far, so good. Now, if the paste appears to be 'hard' you must consider whether a Plymouth, Bristol or New Hall attribution can be ruled out. Her , as always, it will be the characteristics of paste, glaze and decoration that will decide, important points such as the typical spiral wreathing, the dead whiteness of the West Country wares, and the greyness of the inferior New Hall body, with its simple, quickly applied decoration.

In all probability, however, the piece will be soft-paste, English or Welsh. Look again at the translucency. Early Worcester, so creamy white where unprotected by glaze, usually shows greenish, but so does much Liverpool and Longton Hall. In that case remember the careful neatness of Worcester potting, the firecracks and warping, and the candle-fat glaze of Longton, and the thunder-cloud ring of glaze behind so many Liverpool foot-rims. Caughley usually shows straw-yellow or orange, Derby and Chelsea-Derby pale yellow, Lowestoft clear white, and Chelsea greenish yellow with pin-points or moons (depending on period) of greater translucency. As to the glaze, look for Worcester brilliancy and almost invisible bubbling, the dull matt effect of Caughley, and the characteristic Bow green-ness and the brown staining that comes from age.

Every porcelain factory had peculiarities of potting, and the shapes of foot-rims often provide valuable clues. Worcester foot-rims are bluntly triangular in section and so are many Liverpool ones, though others are undercut. Caughley rims are almost invariably rectangular in section, quite deep, and from the small, toy-like Lowestoft rims the paste drops to a point in the centre. Do not be misled by a shrinkage of glaze away from the inner side of the foot-rim, which is a characteristic not peculiar to Worcester, as was once thought. The most that can be said is that it is found more on Worcester pieces than on those of any other factory. A 'biting snake' handle always

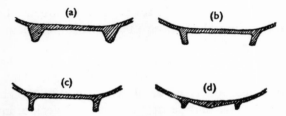

Figure 40. Some typical foot-rim sections. (*a*) Worcester; (*b*) Liverpool;
(*c*) Caughley; (*d*) Lowestoft.

means Liverpool, but a heart-shaped lower handle terminal was used both there and at Bow. Longton Hall scrolled handles cannot be mistaken. In general, no porcelain is so neatly potted as Worcester, none so toy-like as Lowestoft. Of the Welsh porcelains one can say only that the incomparable paste and glaze, once seen and carefully studied, can never be forgotten. But never forget—is it Coalport?

Identification by means of decoration may often be misleading, although broadly speaking the styles of the nineteenth-century porcelains, allied to the monotonous, pure white, highly translucent, standardized bone-ash paste serve to separate them from the earlier wares. All the early decorators copied from the same sources, from the Chinese, from Meissen, and from Sèvres, and the collector has to learn to recognize individual adaptations.

Nevertheless, the typical famille-rose palette of Bow can be easily recognized, as can the Worcester scale-patterns. Learn to know the Chelsea mazarine-blue and the Longton Hall 'Littler's Blue', the Derby 'Japans', the Coalport imitations of Sèvres, and the Rockingham vignetted landscapes.

My readers may have wondered why so little has so far been said about marks. In the first place, they are so numerous that a book of marks is a first essential in every collector's library, and an attempt to list even the commonest in a book of this kind

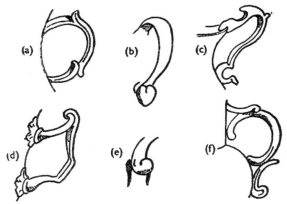

Figure 41. Some typical handles. (*a*) Longton Hall; (*b*) Bow; (*c*) Liverpool; (*d*) Bristol/Worcester; (*e*) Lowestoft; (*f*) Worcester.

would be a waste of time and space. A mark, moreover, should only be considered as the last conclusive proof of origin, in support of other cumulative evidence. It is the last factor to be taken into account, Marks were so often copied. The Meissen crossed-swords mark was copied at Worcester, and re-copied at Lowestoft where the crescent also was often used. Chinese symbols, some of them very like each other, were used at Worcester, Bow, Lowestoft and Caughley, and other foreign marks were copied by many English factories. Nevertheless nineteenth-century marks are usually reliable, and they were, of course, in fairly common use, whereas eighteenth-century porcelain often has no mark at all. Remember too that impressed marks, as used at Swansea and Nantgarw, may often be so filled with glaze that they easily escape notice.

The foregoing remarks are of course intended only as an indication as to the procedure which leads to the arrival at an attribution. The more data, the more knowledge that a collector has gathered together by reading and by examination of pieces, the more accurate that attribution will be, and experience will enable him to arrive more quickly at a decision. At the same time, there are 'puzzle pieces' which have contradictory features, or which resemble nothing that one has seen before. Such are the delight of every collector, and such give rise to conflicting opinion, even between experts.

CHAPTER TWENTY-FOUR

Making a collection

THIS chapter is intended to help a beginner in collecting to derive the utmost enjoyment from his collection, if indeed such an aim can be anything but presumptuous. It would clearly be quite wrong, and in any case impossible, to try to force one's own tastes or preferences upon another, for beauty is above all things subjective. On the other hand, granted that a decision has been reached as to what sort of ware to collect, either by trial and error, or as the result of a long-felt admiration for some particular kind of pottery or porcelain, the pleasure that a collector has in looking at his cabinets can undoubtedly be much enhanced if he cares to take a little trouble with their contents. Mere passive admiration is not really enough.

If there were no art in display there would be no need for any window-dressers. A crowded cabinet is an eyesore, and indeed a real danger. The best kind of cabinet is shallow from front to back, but a deeper one can be improved by making long, light cardboard boxes, covered with suitable material, which can be placed at the back to make additional shelving space. Plates may be leaned against them. China of any kind should have a suitable background, whether plain or patterned is a matter of opinion, but colour is important. Buff-coloured linen is good, and strangely enough so is green, even for 'blue and white', while yellow is essential for the proper display of black basalts. Black is unsatisfactory. There is difference of opinion as to the respective merits of glass or wooden shelves. Wood is safer, and if glass is preferred it should be fairly heavy plate, supported by brackets at close intervals. Plates leaned against the back of a cabinet will slip on glass, and must be placed in stands. These are obtainable in various styles, but the best (and the cheapest) are made of stiff white plastic or rubber-covered wire. Some are fixed, and others are adjustable, and there are sizes for dishes, plates, and cups and saucers.

Cabinet illumination of some kind, preferably switched on simultaneously from the doorway of the room, is most desirable. Strip lighting hidden behind the door-frames is ideal, since when the doors are closed it does not dazzle, the source being invisible. Alternatively, if a cabinet is glass-shelved, a single lamp in a reflector, fixed inside to the cabinet top, will be quite adequate. It is inadvisable to keep the lighting switched on for too long a period with the doors closed, because there is just a possibility that the heat might crack a specimen. A piece of porcelain is highly stressed, which explains why it is impossible to persuade a piece broken out of a bowl to go back exactly into place. The stress was relieved by the break, and the shape of the bowl has changed.

Blue-painted and printed wares do not live happily with polychrome ones, and even the latter can be better displayed if a little thought is given to colour. Thus, nothing looks better than a shelf of Worcester scale-blue, but a piece painted mostly in rouge-de-fer clashes badly with it. Similarly, Japan patterns look best apart from other styles, though it is not necessary to devote an entire shelf to any one class of ware. Some thought should be given to arrangement by size and shape. Plates and dishes make an effective background to smaller pieces, and cups and saucers alternate happily with cream jugs, sucriers or tea-poys. Baskets painted inside should be placed on low shelves, but bowls look really well only when placed up high. On any particular shelf taller pieces should be placed at the ends—a happy mouth turns up at the corners.

Before any piece is placed in the cabinet it should be thoroughly washed in lukewarm water in which an egg-cupful of Scrubb's Ammonia and a squirt of some detergent such as Quix have been well mixed. This solution will effectively remove the dirt from tiny scratches in the glaze. When properly dried the piece may then be polished with a smear of good furniture polish. Never try to dry a figure. Instead, rinse with clear water, and stand it aside to dry of its own accord. A stiff hogshair brush should be used to clear the crevices.

Proper labelling and cataloguing add much to the pleasure of collecting. Self-adhesive labels are excellent, provided that one is willing to replace them when washing needs to be done. Otherwise they may be waterproofed by the application of a coat of transparent acetone-based varnish, such as Cellure. The labels should bear a catalogue number, a description—WORCESTER, BOW and so on—and a date of manufacture. Some add a cachet

Figure 42. Bad and good shelf arrangement.

to their collections by using printed labels—THE JOHN BROWN COLLECTION, for example.

A good catalogue, preferably loose-leaved, will provide space for reference number, attribution, description, mark, date, when and where purchased, cost price and, if possible, a photograph or sketch. Old copies of the *Connoisseur* contain innumerable tiny photographs, in the advertisement pages, which are ideal for the purpose. Alternatively, it is possible to keep a separate photograph album. A great deal of enjoyment may be obtained from photographing one's specimens, for which purpose an old quarter-plate camera on a tripod is ideal. My old Sanderson has served me very well. It does not matter if the lens is slow, since the piece will not move. In order to obtain good definition

of both the front and back edges of a bowl or a tea-pot, stop
well down, and give a long exposure, preferably in daylight and
out of doors, thereby avoiding troublesome reflections and
highlights. If artificial light has to be used, obstinate highlights
may be lessened by dabbing the piece with a lump of putty, or
with a piece of cloth rubbed against a moist cake of soap. Photograph only one specimen at a time, because otherwise the shapes
of those at the sides of a group will tend to be distorted.

Every collector would like to think that his specimens include
none that are forgeries or fakes, and none imperfect. Only the
richer collector will be likely to encounter such forgeries as
'apple-green' Worcester with the green ground added at some
later date, foreign copies of the rarer models of the Toby Jug,
and so on, but there are others which constitute a real danger to
all, against which the only safeguard is long experience. Sampson
figures, usually imitating Derby models, usually betray themselves by their cold brilliance and over-prominent, boldly
enamelled mark, often in the wrong place, but a modern forger
has issued some remarkably good copies of early Chelsea, Derby
and Bow figures that even now are deceiving expert dealers.
Beware of modern Staffordshire cottages, cats, and silver or
pink-lustred jugs and mugs, which are much too brilliant, and
show no signs of age. Remember that at Coalport very good
imitations were made of Chelsea 'goat and bee' jugs, coloured
and white, whose cold, white paste and bright enamels are far
removed from the mellow creaminess and subdued colouring of
the originals. Never buy an expensive, doubtful piece without
calling in expert opinion. It may be found in a junk-shop, but
even junk-shops are combed regularly by knowledgeable dealers.
Look with suspicion upon any piece the underside of which
bears smoky-looking staining, which is usually a sign of
re-decoration.

A broken piece never gives lasting satisfaction. On the other
hand, if an otherwise fine specimen has very slight damage, such
as a missing knob to its cover, or a handle which has 'sprung'
at one terminal, then it may be a wise thing to have it repaired,

for the modern restorer can make an invisible, lasting repair. For this reason it is essential to examine any proposed purchase for this kind of work. Under an ultra-violet lamp, now possessed by most reputable specialists, any repair will show chalky white, but failing this there are still certain tests which are easily made. The original glaze cannot as yet be exactly imitated, the substitute is softer, duller, never so lustrous. By transmitted light a new piece, or a camouflaged crack, is revealed by a denser translucency. Above all, bite the suspected part gently. The original paste and glaze will feel hard, whereas any repaired or 'sprayed' portion will feel soft, even though the teeth do not actually make any impression upon it.

In closing this last chapter, and at the risk of boring repetition, we may sum up by suggesting that collecting can be much more than mere acquisition, which when all is said and done is little more than the sensible use of a good bank balance. Add to such acquisition the pleasures of proper display, cataloguing, photography, discussion with friends of like interests, reading, and visiting the great collections, and the sum total is bound to afford a lifetime of fascinating, utterly absorbing interest and joy.

Bibliography

A LIBRARY of reference books is essential to every collector, whether beginner or expert. This short bibliography is offered only as a suggested nucleus, for so much depends upon personal taste and interest. It can be supplemented at will, for hardly a month passes by without the publication of a new book, or of some book-dealer's list of secondhand copies of old ones. With few necessary exceptions, the most expensive books have been omitted; most are up to date, but certain older ones, often unreliable as regards attribution, have been included either because they are well illustrated, or because nothing better has yet been written.

PORCELAIN

General

Burton, W., *Porcelain, its Nature, Art and Manufacture*, 1906.

Cook, C., *Life and Work of Robert Hancock*, 1948.

Fisher, S. W., *China Collector's Guide*, 1959. *Decoration of English Porcelain*, 1954.

Godden, G. A., *Victorian Porcelain*, 1961.

Honey, W. B., *Old English Porcelain*, 1928.

Jewitt, L., *Ceramic Art of Great Britain*, 1878.

Turner, W., *Transfer Printing on Enamels, Porcelain and Pottery*, 1907.

Specialist

Barrett, F. A., *Worcester Porcelain*, 1953. *Caughley and Coalport Porcelain*, 1951.

Bemrose, G., *Nineteenth Century English Pottery and Porcelain*, 1952.

Boney, K., *Liverpool Porcelain*, 1957.

Fisher, S. W., *English Blue and White Porcelain of the Eighteenth Century*, 1947.

Gilhespy, F. B., *Derby Porcelain*, 1961.

Hayden, A., *Spode and His Successors*, 1925.

Hobson, R. L., *Worcester Porcelain*, 1910.

Hurlbutt, F., *Bow Porcelain*, 1926. *Bristol Porcelain*, 1928. *Chelsea China*, 1937.

John, W. D., *Nantgarw Porcelain*, 1948. *Swansea Porcelain*, 1958.

Mackenna, F. S., *Champion's Bristol Porcelain*, 1947. *Cookworthy's Plymouth and Bristol Porcelain*, 1946. *Chelsea Porcelain: Triangle and Raised Anchor Wares*, 1948. *Chelsea Porce-*

lain: The Red Anchor Period, 1951. *Chelsea Porcelain: The Gold Anchor Period*, 1952.

Marshall, H. R., *Coloured Worcester Porcelain of the First Period*, 1954.

Ruscoe, W., *English Porcelain Figures*, 1947.

Watney, B., *Longton Hall Porcelain*, 1957.

EARTHENWARE

General

Bemrose, G., *Nineteenth Century English Pottery and Porcelain*, 1952.

Haggar, R. G., *English Country Pottery*, 1950.

Hayden, A., *Chats on English Earthenware*, 1909.

Rackham, B., *Early Staffordshire Pottery*, 1951. *Medieval English Pottery*, 1948.

Slipware

Lomax, C. J., *Quaint Old English Pottery*, 1909.

Delft

Downman, E. A., *Blue Dash Chargers*, 1919.

Garner, F. H., *English Delftware*, 1948.

Lustre

John, W. D., *Old English Lustre Pottery*, 1951.

Stoneware

Blacker, J. F., *ABC of English Salt Glaze Stoneware*, 1922.

Cream-ware

Towner, D., *English Cream-coloured Earthenware*, 1957.

Figures

Andrade, C., *Astbury Figures*, 1924.

Haggar, R. G., *English Pottery Figures*, 1947.

Wedgwood

Barnard, H., *Chats on Wedgwood Ware*, 1924.

Church, A. H., *Josiah Wedgwood*, 1908.

Honey, W. B., *Wedgwood Ware*, 1948.

MARKS

Thorn, C. J., *Handbook of Old Pottery and Porcelain Marks*, 1947.

Index